CONTENTS

# BEGONE GODMEN!

## ENCOUNTERS WITH SPIRITUAL FRAUDS

**DR. ABRAHAM KOVOOR**

Edited by
V. A. MENON

JAICO PUBLISHING HOUSE

Ahmedabad Bangalore Chennai
Delhi Hyderabad Kolkata Mumbai

Published by Jaico Publishing House
A-2 Jash Chambers, 7-A Sir Phirozshah Mehta Road
Fort, Mumbai - 400 001
jaicopub@jaicobooks.com
www.jaicobooks.com



BEGONE GODMEN!
Encounters with Spiritual Frauds
ISBN 81-7224-331-6

First Jaico Impression: 1976
Seventh Jaico Impression: 1998



Printed by
Trinity Academy For Corporate Training Limited, Mumbai

## FOREWORD

### *DR. KOVOOR—THE MILITANT ICONOCLAST*

Dr. Abraham T. Kovoor, the world-renowned rationalist and psychiatrist, **was** an outstanding scientist who had conducted intensive researches for over half a century into all types of alleged psychic, para-psychic and spiritual phenomena, and came to the conclusion that there is absolutely no objective truth behind such claims and beliefs. He **was** the first and the only scientist among psychical researchers in the world who was awarded a doctorate for his work in this field. The Minnesota Institute of Philosophy of U.S. awarded him a doctorate for his thesis on psychic and para-psychic phenomena. His contention is that all those who claim to possess psychic, para-psychic and spiritual powers are either hoaxers or mentally deranged persons suffering from Cryptesthesia He says, "nobody has and nobody ever had supernatural powers. They exist only in the pages of scriptures and sensation-mongering newspapers."

Dr. Kovoor had been the only Asian scientist who was invited by the Ernst Haeckel Ecology Centre of U.S. to join the team of scientists in the "Haeckel Expedition" to the Indian Ocean and its litoral countries for collecting matter to fill the gaps in the organic evolution ladder. But his wife's prolonged illness and eventual death forced Dr. Kovoor to decline this invitation.

Dr. Kovoor was widely travelled,and had delivered public lectures in many countries and world conferences. Stories from his Case Book were and are serialised in newspapers and magazines in various countries. One of the stories from his Case Book was filmed in Malayalam. Tamil and Telugu. "NAMBIKKAI" a Tamil Drama, which was staged several times before packed audiences; is also based on another story from his Case Book.

Dr. Kovoor, who had a life-long mission to teach people to go by reason and not by superstition, was born at

Tiruvalla in Kerala on 10th April, 1898 as the son of the late Very Rev. Kovoor Eipe Thomma Katthanar, the Vicar General of the Mar Thomma Syrian Church of Malabar. In his opening address in the film "PUNAR-JANMAM", where he appears in his own role as a psychiatrist, Dr. Kovoor comments about his birth thus:

"Over three quarters of a century ago I was born in the beautiful land of Kerala in a Syrian Christian family as the son of a christian priest as the result of a geographical and biological accident, over which I had neither control nor choice. But when I came of mature age I adopted an equally beautiful country—Sri Lanka—as my country, and rationalism as my philosophy as the result of my volitional act."

After completing his school education at the Syrian Christian Seminary, Tiruvalla, started by his father first at his ancestral home, and later moved on to a dominant site in the town donated by him to the Church. Dr. Kovoor, with his younger brother the late Dr. Behanan T. Kovoor, formerly of the Yale University U.S.A., and the United Nations, proceeded to Calcutta for higher education. At Bengabasi College, Calcutta, he specialised in botany and zoology.

After two years' service as Assistant Lecturer in botany at the C.M.S. College, Kottayam, Dr. Kovoor migrated to Sri Lanka in 1928 at the invitation of Rev. P. T. Cash, the principal of Jaffna Central College. Rev. Cash, an outstanding botanist, met Dr. Kovoor at Ooty while both of them were out in the field collecting specimens of mountain flora.

During his first year at Jaffna Central College young Kovoor was asked to teach scripture to the final year students in addition to botany. When the results came from the Cambridge University it was found that all his students passed in scripture with credits and distinctions. Next year there was no scripture in Kovoor's time-table. It was given over to Rev. O. L. Gibbon, the Vice-Principal. When questioned about it, Rev. Cash said with a smile in, his face, "Abraham, I know you produced the best result in scripture. All your students passed in scripture, but all of them lost their religions!"

Leaving Jaffna Central College in 1943, when Rev. Cash retired and left Sri Lanka, Dr. Kovoor joined Richmond College, Galle, and later St. Thomas College, Mount Lavinia. In 1959 he retired from service as the head of the seience department at Thurstan College, Colomoo.

It was only after retirement from service that Dr. Kovoor began to speak and write about his life-long research into the field of spiritualism and psychic phenomena. "Like all children I was indoctrinated and brain-washed in the superstitious beliefs and practices of my parents' religion, and it was an up-hill task for me to get rid of those foolish notions in my adulthood", says Dr. Kovoor. To avoid repeating the same mistake Dr. Kovoor decided not to indoctrinate their only son—Dr. Aries Kovoor with absurd ideas in the name of religion. Professor Aries Kovoor, who at present is directing scientific researches under the French and Cuban governments, is bringing up nis three sons without any trace of religious beliefs. For this, Aries has the full co-operation of his intellectual wife Prof. Jacquiline Kovoor.

The obituary notice of Dr. Kovoor's wife, who died in November 1974 created a big sensation in Sri Lanka, even in the Island's parliament. The obituary reads, "Mrs. Acca KoVoor expired leaving behind neither a mind nor a 'spirit' to bother credulous people. According to her wish her body will be removed to the Faculty of Medicine, University of Sri Lanka, Colombo, from Tiruvalla, Pamankada Lane, Colombo-6, today (Friday) at 8 a.m. No funeral, no cremation and no flowers."

Though this obituary notice was published in all the local newspapers, the Sri Lanka Broadcasting Corporation refused to include it in the list of obituary broadcasts When the question was raised in the parliament, the , Minister of Broadcasting, who happened to be a Roman Catholic, stated that the rejection was based on the opinions expressed by a Roman Catholic priest and a Buddhist monk. It is rather strange that a Buddhist monk who believes in the "anathma" doctrine of Buddha shared the belief of the Catholic priest that man has a soul in his "sacred heart"!

Mrs. Kovoor was a pillar of strength to her husband in his researches and activities. She was the Treasurer of the Sri Lanka Rationalist Association from the time of its inception, and attended world conferences of free-thinkers with her husband.

As an investigator of so-called occult phenomena Dr. Kovoor had busied himself in removing from the minds of ignorant people their unfounded fear about ghosts, and debunking the claims of miracle performers, charmists, astrologers, palmists, spiritualists, numerologists, necromancists and all other types of charlatans who hoodwink the gullibles by claiming occult and spiritual powers. He had slept in haunted houses and walked in cemeteries in search of ghosts. He had commenced the most important events of his life at inauspicious moments. To convince the ignorant masses that all those who claim miraculous powers are pure hoaxers or mentally sick persons, he had thrown out the following permanent challenge against them.

THE CHALLENGE

"I, Abraham T. Kovoor of 'Tiruvalla', Pamankada Lane, Colombo-6, do hereby state that I am prepared to pay an award of one lakh Sri Lanka rupees to any one from any part of the world who can demonstrate supernatural or miraculous powers under fraud-proof conditions. This offer will remain open till my death, or till I find the first "winner.

Godmen, saints, yogis, sidhas, gurus, swamis and all others who claim that they have acquired miraculous powers through spiritual exercises or divine boons, can win this award if they can perform any one of the following "miracles".

1. Read the serial number of a sealed-up currency note.
2. Produce an exact replica of a currency note.
3. Stand stationary on burning cinders for half a minute without blistering the feet with the help of his god.
4. Materialise from nothing an object I ask
5. Move or bend a solid object using psychokinetic power.
6. Read the thought of another person using telepathic powers.
7. Make an amputated limb grow even one inch by prayer, spiritual powers, Lourdes water, holy ash blessing etc.

8. Levitate in the air by yogic power.
9. Stop the heart-beat for five minutes by yogic power.
10. Walk on water.
11. Leave the body in one place and materialize in another place.
12. Stop breathing for thirty minutes by yogic power.
13. Develop creative intelligence or get enlightened through transcendental or any other type of meditation.
14. Speak an unknown language as a result of rebirth or by being possessed by holy or evil spirit.
15. Produce a spirit or ghost to be photographed.
16. Disappear from a film when photographed.
17. Get out of a locked room by divine power.
18. Increase the quantity by weight of a substance.
19. Detect a hidden object.
20. Convert water into petrol or wine.
21. Convert wine into blood.
22. Astrologers and palmists who hoodwink the gullibles by claiming that astrology and palmistry are scientific, can win my award if they can pick out correctly—within a margin of five per cent error—those of males, females, the living and the dead from a set of ten palm prints or ten astrological charts giving the exact time of birth correct to the minute, and places of birth with their latitudes and longitudes.

This challenge is governed by the following conditions:—

1. The person who takes up the challenge, whether he wants my award or not, should deposit with my nominee or myself an earnest deposit of Rs. 1000. I insist on this deposit, which will be refunded in the event of his winning the test, just to keep away those bent on cheap publicity who would only waste my time, money and energy.
2. A person will be considered an acceptor of the challenge only after he makes the earnest deposit, and no correspondence will be made with anyone who fails to do so.

3. After the earnest deposit is made, the claim of the person will first be tested by my nominee in public on a mutually agreed day.
4. If the person fails to face the test or loses in the preliminary test, his deposit will be forfeited.
5. If the person wins the preliminary test, I will personally conduct the final test in public.
6. If a person wins the final test, his deposit will be refunded together with my award of one lakh rupees.
7. All tests will be conducted under fraud-proof conditions to the fullest satisfaction of myself or my nominee.

Although Dr. Kovoor threw out this challenge twelve years ago in 1963, and was published all over the world, nobody was able to win one cent from, him. Copies of his challenge were sent to the numerous astrologers, palmists, godmen and godwomen of India prior to his two "Divine Miracle Exposure Campaign" throughout the length and breadth of India in 1975. Only one doctor in Bangalore was foolhardy to take up the challenge and made the earnest deposit. The net result was that Dr. Kovoor went back to Sri Lanka after the lecture campaign richer by Rs. 1000!

Dr. Kovoor had been a terror to those who cheat innocent and gullible masses in the garb of holy men or miracle performers. His fervour to wipe out superstition from the face of earth, and establish a humanitarian tradition makes Dr. Kovoor one of the noblest personalities of the twentieth century.

This book is the materialisation of a longing desire of mine to share with others some of his thought-provoking articles. This book which contains some of the best of Dr. Kovoor's writings, will surely be an eye-opener to those who believe in the supernatural, the miraculous and the spiritual.

Bombay. V. A. Menon

# PREFACE

Sincere and honest persons earn their living by sincere and honest work. Dishonest persons do so by cheating those who work and earn. To the category of dishonest parasites who thrive by cheating the credulous among honest workers belong the teachers, preachers and priests of dubious religions and cults; mystics, saints, arahants and sidhas who claim that they have acquired enlightenment through meditation or penance; gurus, babas, anandas, rishis, swamijis and yogis who claim that they have obtained miraculous powers through yogic practices or as boons from gods; oracles, exorcists, charmers, soothsayers, fortune tellers and all types of occultists who claim that they have developed their special powers through spiritual exercises, astrology, palmistry, numerology, telepathy, clairvoyance, telekinesis (Psychokinesis), precognition, necromancy, spirit possession etc.

In recent years a new type of hoaxers have cropped up in India in the form of incarnations of one or other of numerous gods of the Hindu pantheon. Intelligent crooks of that country have found a new method of amassing wealth with the least effort. They get hold of a person who is clever at sleight-of-hand tricks, and brand him as an 'avathar'. A lot of cock-and-bull stories about the miraculous genesis and divine powers of the godman, are published in books and newspapers. Whenever this imitation of god appears in public, his agents offer him flowers and prostrate before him. As most gullibles have the habit of doing exactly as others do, the thousands of credulous spectators too prostrate before the miracle-performing charlatan. Money pours in lakhs to be shared by the juggler and his agents. It is indeed a tragedy that among these crafty god-makers are some of the highly qualified scientists of that country.

Although the acts of these hoaxers are as criminal as those of robbers, cheats, smugglers, blackmarketers, pick-pockets and thieves, governments are reluctant to prosecute them because their practice is sanctioned by most religions. In a democracy where the majority of people are blind believers in religions, these hoaxers can carry on their trade of cheating with impunity.' If legal action is to be taken against them, the first person to be prosecuted will be- the Pope, the earthly representative of Christ, for cheating his gullible flock by making them believe that the wine they are given during the Holy Sacrament is blood of Christ. That this is a fraud can be proved by subjecting the Sacrament Wine to chemical test.

It was to convince the ignorant masses that there is absolutely no truth in the claims of these hoaxers that I have been challenging them staking all I have to demonstrate their powers under **fraud**-proof conditions.

I am aware that my various challenges, staking large sums of money, are liable to create a false impression in the minds of the public that I am a fabulously rich man with plenty of money to throw about for cheap publicity. I am also aware of the dire consequences of these challenges. If there is one person in the world with supernatural or paranormal powers, I will eventually have to end up in a Home for Destitutes. But I was, and still am, fully confident that I will not be losing a single cent by these challenges, because nobody has, and nobody ever had, miraculous powers although we read in scriptures and sensation-mongering newspapers numerous stories about people possessing miraculous powers. That is why I am keeping these challenges open till my death or till I find the first winner.

None of the hoaxers who claim supernatural powers will dare to take up my challenge for fear of their fraud getting exposed under scientific tests. The only person who was foolhardy to deposit Rs. 1000|- as proof of his earnestness to face my challenge, was, strangely enough, not one of the charlatans, but a highly religious person who blindly believed in the supernatural and the miraculous.

Dr. G. Venkata Rao, a medical doctor of Bangalore, who was credulous enough to believe that his Guru Raghavendra Swamiji of Mantralaya, Andhra Pradesh, has divine powers, paid Rs. 1000 as earnest deposit, and finally lost it!

Dr. Rao foolishly believed that a person could obtain divine powers by chanting the manthra "Om Raghavendra Sharanam" daily 100 times. Being an extremely gullible person he also believed the cock-and-bull story that sacred ash, honey and flowers come out like fountain from the eye of a 6-year-old child in a village in Mysore district.

Later, getting wiser—probably after testing the claim of the miracle child himself at my request—he wanted his deposit returned. Much against my wish, I had to decline his request as it was against the conditions of my challenge.

I am extremely glad that Mr. V. A. Menon is bringing out this book for the benefit of the public. It is my earnest hope that his efforts will be helpful in weeding out many of these charlatans, and weaning out the credulous masses from their foolish beliefs in the supernatural and the miraculous.

Dr. Abraham T. Kovoor

"Thiruvalla",
Pamankada Lane, Colombo-6.

Dr Kovoor and wife investigating a case.

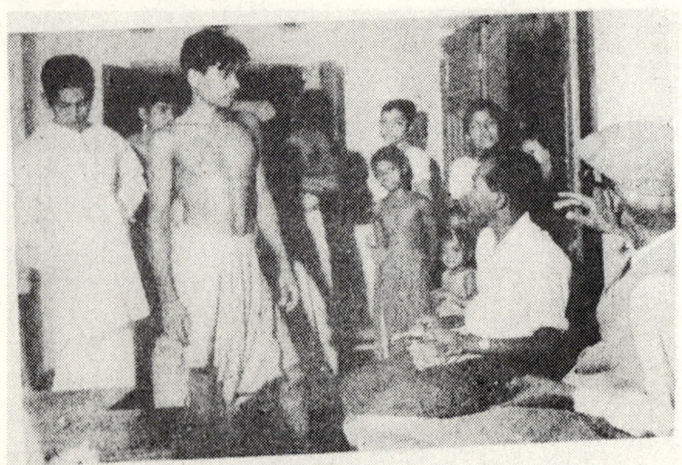

Dr Kovoor investigating a haunted house.

A house that was brought down by a poltergeist.

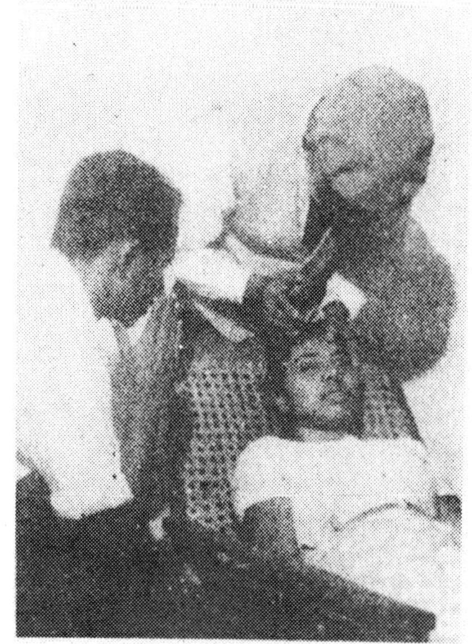

**A poltergeist is being** hypnotised by Dr. Kovoor.

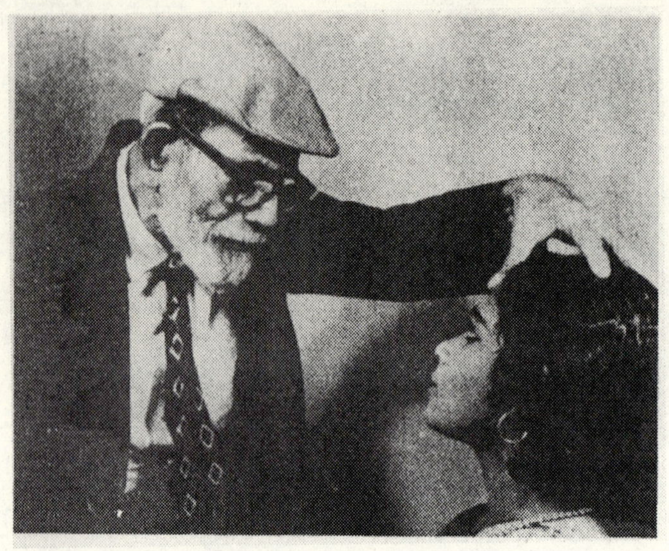

Dr Kovoor's powerful hypnotheraphy.

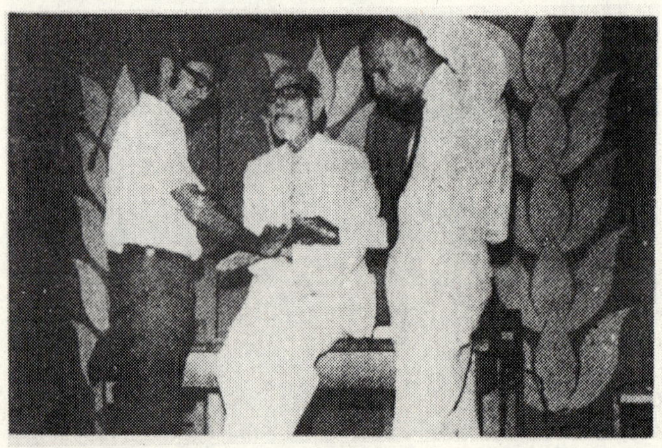

Dr Kovoor stops his pulse while being checked by two doctors.

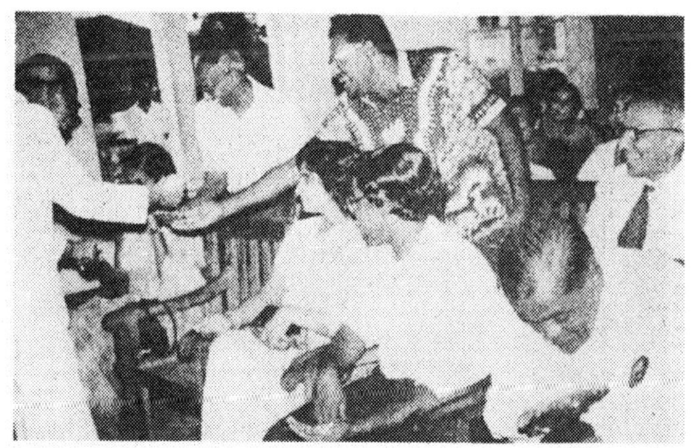

Dr Kovoor distributing "Holy Ash".

Mr Jayasuriya hangs on hooks holding the microphone in hand.

Hanging Jayasuriya flanked by
Dr Abraham T. Kovoor and Dr Carlo Fonseka.

Malayalam wall-poster of the film "PUNAR JANMAM" based on the story "Son and Mother" from Dr Kovoor's casebook.

Dr Kovoor, when he was a student in 1922.

Dr Kovoor with V. K. Krishna Menon.

Dr Kovoor with M. C. Joseph, the late rationalist leader of Kerala.

Dr Kovoor and his wife Mrs Acca Kovoor with former Sri Lanka Prime Minister Smt Sirimavo Bandaranaike.

Dr Kovoor releasing the ist edition of BEGONE GODMEN.

## INTRODUCTION

Dr. Abraham T. Kovoor was a missionary in the true sense of the term: he was supremely committed to make every conceivable effort, even in his ripe old age, to propagate the philosophy he holds dear to his heart—atheism—and convert as many people as possible to his thinking. In order that I am not misunderstood, I hasten to add that Dr. Kovoor's was not a mission to interpret a new dogma to the world:his was a creative mission,the mission of propagating a philosophical world outlook churned out of the milk of modern seience. A philosopher has to be committed, and Dr. Kovoor was committed to atheism in every aspect of his mental life, conscious or unconscious.

Atheism is a negative term, opposed to theism. This is because theism was ruling the roost for the past several centuries, ever since the original naturalism of early man, as expressed in ancient Greek and Indian materialistic philosophies, had to give way for the emergence of the religions, which in the context of the miseries and helplessness of man, postulated the schizophrenic concept of god. But the human intellect, in its development through **Work** and confrontation with nature ultimately rediscovered ,the original materialism at a higher stage since the emergence of science, and got itself strengthened by the practice of productive activity by employing science and technology, and this process has heralded the historic battle between materialism and spiritualism in modern times. Materialism has its own integral social philosophy as explained by Marx, and the battle of ideas is a complex historico-social process that has to go through myriads of vicissitudes. But the trend and thrust of history indicate the only logical result of this battle: the ultimate victory of materialism or atheism over idealism or spiritualism. This is the essence of the ideological battle or the battle of ideas. And Dr. Kovoor had been playing a very eminent role in this battle of ideas in the

Indian subcontinent and Sri Lanka, and his reputation is international.

In the realm of popular life, the battle is waged in concrete terms, not in terms of abstract philosophy. The fight of Dr. Kovoor and his rationalist followers has been against all kinds of superstitions about gods, godmen, exorcists, miracle makers, soothsayers, et al. This battle is very important, for without liberating the masses from these superstitions social progress is impossible. Dr. Kovoor confines himself to this aspect of the problem, and has not ventured into an analysis of the economic and social roots of the continuance of superstitions and the belief in gods and religions. I personally feel that in the ultimate analysis the battle against superstition can succeed only as a part of the battle of proletariat for liberation. In other words the social conditions of alienation which leads to superstitious beliefs as an escape route from the miseries of life have to be abolished.

But the battle of militant materialism must go on and Dr. Kovoor had been an uncompromising commander of the army of committed rationalists, whose undogmatic and creative mission is to expose the hollowness of the claims of godmen and miracle men. This battle undoubtedly helps the cause of human progress.

Bombay —HARIHARAN POONJAR

# Chapter 1

## *THOSE CHALLENGES*

Over fifty years of intensive researches into diverse types of alleged paranormal happenings, and claims of non-existent miraculous powers of mystics, yogis, rishis, sidhas, kattadiyas, charmists, astrologers, palmists, anjanakkarayas, spiritualists etc., I have succeeded in getting rid of many superstitious beliefs I held as a result of indoctrination and brainwashing from childhood, inevitable in the society we live in.

Some of the worst fears of my childhood were about ghosts, charms, curses hell, and the anger of gods and demons. Systematic investigations and rational thinking from my university days made me doubt the veracity of numerous religious myths, occultism, prophetic predictions, immortal spirits, and claims of miracle performers.

In all the hundreds of haunted houses and poltergeistic phenomena I have investigated, I have been able to detect the human agent responsible for the mysterious occurrences. They did such diabolic acts as a result of some kind of mental derangement, or out • of mere mischief. I have cured numerous neurotics supposed to be "possessed", not by driving out the non-existent spirit from them, but by removing through hypnosis such delusions from the unfortunate victims' subconscious minds. I realised that the occasional successes some kattadiyas and religious priests achieve through 'thovil', poojas or prayers are all due to the hypnotic influence of .such cults on the suggestible minds of the patients. Ignorant persons attributed such cures to the gods and demons invoked by the exorcists.

I was also able to realise that the glossolalial (Zenoglossic) talks, even in changed voices, of persons under ecstatic trance were neither due to possession by spirits, nor due to the memories of previous incarnations, but due to wild imaginations of deluded minds.

I have slept in haunted houses. Both myself and my wife have gone at midnight to cemeteries in search of ghosts. I have broadcast over the CBC from Kanatte cemetery at night. Although we did not see any ghost there, had we been deliberately frightened by someone producing some strange sound, we would have suffered severe mental shock , because, though the idea of the existence of ghosts had been fully removed from our conscious minds, it would have still remained hidden in our subconscious minds. On the other hand, had it been our son, who was brought up without any indoctrination about ghosts, demons and gods, except what he read from books and newspapers without our knowledge, he would not have suffered such shocks.

Nearly every one in our midst believes foolishly in auspicious times, lucky numbers, omens, evil eye, evil tongue, lucky colours, lucky gems, charms, astrology, palmistry, light reading, tumbler talks, planchettes, kanappuwa, anjanamelia, card reading, numerology, necromancy, demonology, spiritualism, possession, materialisation, marvellous powers of prayers, poojas, manthras, sacrifices, pilgrimages, offerings to gods, pirith nool, holy ash, crucifix, relics, talisman, sacred places, sacred persons, sacred times, sacred objects, telepathy, clairvoyance, portent of gecko's chirp, dog's howl, owl's hoot and numerous other absurdities.

My investigations made me realise the fact that such delusional beliefs are made to take deep roots in the minds of credulous persons by occultists, theologists, and demonologists, because their source of income depends on such superstitious beliefs of the gullibles. Prayers, poojas, sacrifices, offerings etc., had only psychological influences on credulous believers. They all acted as narcotics on human minds. Desecration of the so-called sacred, and offending of all powerful gods and demons created fear in the gullibles, the root cause of most mental diseases.

From my youth I have been deliberately violating all these man-made superstitious practices to test their effects. I spent two years learning astrology and palmistry, but my study helped me only to discover their futility. I have always selected inauspicious times and bad omens to commence important events in my life, and realised the absurdity of such beliefs. Once I lost a good buyer for a property of mine in India as the date I selected for signing the Sale Deed was inauspicious both for the buyer as well as the seller.

My aged mother was in tears for several days because I stepped out on my left foot on my way to wed.

The foundation stone for my bungalow "Tiruvalla" at Pamankada Lane, Colombo-6, was laid at an inauspicious time, much against the liking of the contractor and the workmen.

I began giving publicity to my researches, and to express my views on diverse types of superstitious beliefs of men, only after my retirement. I refrained from giving expression 10 opinions earlier because of the fact that I had to earn my bread and butter by working in nor secular institutions founded to spread blind beliefs.

Eventually, when I started writing and speaking, there was a deluge of protests from all types of occultists like religious priests, kattadiyas, astrologers, palmists, spiritualists, fortune tellers, telepathists, clairvoyants etc. Some said that they could kill me by their charms. Spiritualists said that they could do harm to me through spirits. Some said that they could show me spirits if I could go with them at night to cemeteries stark naked, and drink a magic potion.

I finally decided that the best way to expose the bluff and fraud of these charlatans was to challenge them to come forward and prove their claims in public under fraud-proof conditions. I was aware that my various challenges staking large sums of money were liable to create a false impression in the minds of the public that I am a fabulously rich man with plenty of money to throw about for the sake of cheap publicity. I was also aware of the dire consequences of these challenges. If there was one person in this world with supernatural powers, I would eventually have to spend my old age in a Home for Destitutes. But I was, and still am, fully confident that I will not be losing a single cent by these bets. That is the reason why I am keeping all my challenges open till my death. It is my wish that my son too will keep these challenges open at least till his finances permit.

My first challenge was issued in June 1963. I waged an amount between Rs. 1,000 and Rs. 25,000—against an equal amount—that no person, whatever his mystical powers, could tell correctly the serial number on a currency note sealed up in an envelope. For the benefit of those who claimed to possess telepathic powers, I was prepared to allow one of the judges to see the number on the said note so that the telepathist in another room could read the judge's mind. It contained a special invitation to Dr. J. B. Rhine of Duke University, an exponent of ESP. In January 1965 the maximum of this wager was raised to Rs. 75,000 to enable occultists from foreign countries to come to Colombo and make a big profit even after spending for their air travel.

In 1966 some kattadiyas in this country said they had the power to read the number of the sealed note, but the amount stipulated in my challenge was too high for them. To satisfy their poor purses the minimum wager was reduced from Rs. 1,000 to Rs. 75.

To spiritualists I threw out a challenge that I would pay Rs. 5,000 to any one who could produce a ghost or demon to be photographed.

To prove astrology is a gamble, I said that I would give the dates of birth, correct to the minute, together with the latitudes and longitudes of places of birth of ten persons. I offered Rs. 1,000 to each astrologer who could tell correctly the sex and dates of death, if dead, of the ten persons, with a margin of error of 5%. To the palmists I said that I would give the palm-prints of the ten persons concerned instead of their dates of birth. To prevent a mad rush of charlatans claiming through newspapers, only to get free publicity, I stipulated a refundable deposit of Rs. 75 from each contestant.

India being a land of Hindus who do everything in their lives only after consulting astrologers, two Indian newspapers undertook to conduct this test on my behalf. B. V. Raman and several other "professors of Astrology" in that country were sent press cuttings of this challenge. But so far, not a single astrologer in any part of the world had the courage to take up my challenge by depositing the minimum of Rs. 75.

On three occasions I challenged all charmists in this country through the Sinhalese, Tamil and English newspapers to kill me during stipulated periods by their charms or vas kavis. On all the three occasions I have been receiving numerous charms by post. Till today I have received anonymously about 50 charms, some on copper and silver foils and the rest *on* ola and paper. In spite of all these charms sent by kattadiyas from all parts of the Island, I am still hale and hearty. Eventually when I die, as all humans do, these charlatans might say that I died as a result of the delayed action of their charms!

In 1970, in reply to the "President of the Kataragama Devotees Association" I offered a reward of Rs. 100,000 to any one who could stand on fire for 30 seconds without getting burnt. The contestant was required to make a refundable deposit of Rs. 1,000.

Although none of the claimants of various paranormal powers came forward to take up my challenge by depositing the stipulated amounts, there were several who said that they had no money to make the deposit, but still claimed supernatural powers. Even though I should not have taken them seriously as they were not even prepared to stake the minimum amount stipulated, I invited many to come forward and exhibit their powers in public free under fraud-proof conditions. Except for the two following persons who were fool hardy to face my test, all others failed to turn up at the last moment:

One Mr. Neville de Silva wrote in the "Times of Ceylon" that he had telepathic powers, and that he was prepared to prove it to me if I was prepared to test his power. On 15th August, 1967 a test was conducted in the office of the Times of Ceylon in the presence of its editors. Out of the seven answers given by Mr. Neville de Silva, not a single one was right!

A fortune telling clairvoyant Mr. C. D. Edusooriya of Waskaduwa, who claimed Prime Ministers, Ministers, Parliamentarians and VIPs among his clients, volunteered to read the serial number on a currency note kept sealed up in the safe custody of the Editor of 'Dawasa' He wanted several days to find an auspicious day to conduct a pooja to make him clairvoyant. Finally when the number he produced was compared with the number on the note in the editor's safe, it was found to be utterly wrong!

Numerous fools in India and Ceylon worship certain jugglers like Sathya Sai Baba, Pandrimalai Swamigal, Neelakanda Swamigal, Dattabal, Dadaji and Acharya Rajneesh of India as incarnations of God because these charlatans claim that they can materialise objects such as Holy ash, Lingam etc., from nowhere by their divine powers. Since there were numerous articles in newspapers about their miraculous powers written by their gullible devotees, I had to challenge them to produce any object from 'nowhere' after I search their bodies. If they had any objection in an "unholy" man like me touching their 'sacred' bodies, I said that I would be satisfied if they could materialise a replica of a currency note I would be showing them. Although these challenges were conveyed to them through Indian Newspapers, and registered letters direct to them, these so-called Bhagawans have not yet responded.

One of the strong arguments of those who are out to show that there are scientific evidence to prove rebirth, is to cite reported cases of persons talking about their so-called previous life under hypnotic regression. Persons like the late Prof. K. N. Jayatilleke went to the extent of saying that even physical and physiological changes could be brought about by hypnotic regression.

To prove the absurdity of the above mistaken notion, I challenged hypnotists offering a reward of any amount between Rs. 75 and Rs. 75,000 on a reciprocal basis, to hypnotically regress identical twins separately to their "pre-natal life" and make them narrate identical descriptions of their common "previous life".

To those who claimed that they could bring about physiological changes by hypnotic regression, I challenged any hypnotist to hypnotise an expectant mother, and regress her to her pre-conception period, and make the foetus in her womb disappear. A similar challenge was issued to those who claimed that subjects under hypnosis could be made clairvoyant.

## SOME CHARLATANS

One Buddhist monk Rev. Walagedara Indusumana Thero published through a Sinhalese newspaper that he could produce a ghost to be photographed according to my challenge. After my acceptance of this was published in the same newspaper, there was no response from him.

One Mr. Nandris de Silva, a kattadiya from Panadura claimed through the columns of Silumina that he could put a ghost into my palm, show a demon in a mirror, get me stuck to the chair on which I was seated, and get all the furniture in my bungalow smashed up with the help of ghosts and demons under his control Though several dates were fixed, both by the editor of Silumina and myself Mr. Nandris de Silva to demonstrate his 'powers', he never appeared.

In 1969 one Dr. M.H.M. Nazeem of Watawala, who claimed himself to be a spiritualist, wrote me the following letter:—

"Regarding evidence of spirits, I am prepared to effectively demonstrate the manifestations of spirits on any day, except on poya days, between the sunset and dawn. This challenge is only to the members of your rationalist association, and not for public display.. . One of you shall light an oil lamp or a candle in a room with all other lights off, and come out after locking the door with key. All present, including me, shall remain outside the locked room. Within five minutes the locked door will open on its own, simultaneously the lamp or the candle being extinguished. After about ten minutes, the lamp or the candle will relight on its own, and the door will lock itself again. If there is an expensive lamp hanging from the ceiling, I will cause it to be dashed to the floor in the vacant room. If you are interested, please let me know about three weeks in advance."

I invited Dr. Nazeem by registered letter to come to my residence on 22nd November, 1969 to demonstrate his powers before some judges and journalists. He accepted the invitation.

About this spiritualist's failure to turn up on the appointed date, the Times of Ceylon' wrote under the caption "A Walkover for Mr. Kovoor" thus: —

"He never came, so we never saw; and Ceylon's ace rationalist Abraham Kovoor got a walk-over."

"He, a doctor from Watawala — was the latest to take up Kovoor's challenge to prove that spirits exist. He, according to protracted correspondence with Mr. Kovoor, had promised to stage a demonstration at Kovoor's Wellawatta house between 7 and 9 p.m. on a Saturday."

"We were the eager audience waiting to witness the demonstration. Among us were a Methodist minister, two university dons and two journalists."

In January 1969, the Times Weekender came out with a challenge to me on the front page by an anonymous person saying that "he is prepared to show me the powers of God and unseen powers if I would go to the Kelaniya Buddhist temple. I replied that I am prepared to take up the challenge provided the challenger is prepared to divulge his identity".

Without either divulging his identity or getting permission from the temple authorities, he announced through the "Times Weekender" that he would be coming "in the name of God" under the Makarathorana of Kelaniya temple on March 3rd at 8 a.m.

Though a fairly large crowd assembled that morning at the temple to see the challenger "coming in the name of God to demonstrate the powers of unseen God and spirits", he never appeared on the scene. Later investigations revealed that the anonymous challenger was a European skin diver, turned film producer and director, who became a psychopath due to narcotic drugs.

Siri Kempitia of Kegalle, one Gamage of Boralasgamuwa, and S. P. Vancuylenberg of Kelaniya are the astrologers who agreed to come to Thurstan College Hall to face my test on astrology but failed to turn up on the appointed dates.

One Ranawaka of Abekolawewa claimed through the columns of Silumina that he had a baby at home whose photos taken by various persons always showed a snake and a sword on either side of the child's picture.

Through the same paper I invited Mr. Ranawaka to bring the child to Colombo to be photographed. Although I offered to meet all the expenses for bringing the child to Colombo, there was no response from him. Finally two members of the Ceylon Rationalist Association went all the way to Abekolawewa with cameras to photograph the miracle child. But when they went there, they were not even allowed to see the child. The neighbours told them that it was all a big hoax on the part of Ranawaka to attract people to his household Devale with their "offerings".

◆

A special meeting of the Ceylon Rationalist Association was held on 11th July, 1970 at the request of a member Mr. S. Thirunavukkarasu, Electrical Engineer, Badula, to enable a miracle-performing devotee of Sai Baba from

Bandarawela to demonstrate his Siddi powers by performing miracles before our members. Although this 'swami' undertook to accompany Mr. Thirunavukkarasu to Colombo, he disappeared from Bandarawala the previous night with one of his women devotees.

Though this charlatan disappointed hundreds of spectators that day, one of our members Mr. D. W. Chandrasena, an expert magician and a member of the Ceylon Magic Circle, entertained the spectators with numerous Sai Baba tricks. According to an ex-devotee of Sai Baba, the quantity of Holy Ash Mr. Chandrasena produced that day was much more than what Sai Baba used to produce before his devotees.

Onc C. Ganeswaran, identified as a clerk at the Bank of Ceylon, Kandy told me over the telephone that he could prove to me the power of charms by causing damage to my forefinger. I invited him to do so at the Rationalist Association meeting. Although he agreed to come and demonstrate it, he never turned up!

One C. C. C. Gunaseelan of the TW & OP Office, General Treasury, Colombo, boasted through the Ceylon Daily News that he is capable of reading the number on a sealed up currency note. He too failed to appear to demonstrate his powers on the appointed date. Another person who boasted through the newspaper, "Rivirasa" that he could read the number on the currency note was the Buddhist monk Gnanasisi Thero of Mirihana. Even after repeated requests, he too backed out. Arthur Jinadasa, a kattadiya from Beliatta was another clairvoyant who claimed to have the power of reading the number on the sealed currency note, but disappeared at the last moment.

M. Mohotti of Kelaniya and Lionel Gamage of Mahabulankulama announced through newspapers that they were prepared to take up my challenge to stand on fire for 30 seconds without getting burnt. Mohotti was asked to make a deposit of Rs. 1,000 to prove that he is in earnest. He never came forward after that. Since Lionel Gamage said that he had no money, I agreed to test his claim free at the Thurstan College grounds. Since the Education Department withdrew the permission to conduct the test at Thurstan College, the venue was changed to the Head Quarters of the G.C.S.U. but Gamage did not come.

After about four months, news reached me that Gamage was having roaring practice in fortune-telling through palmistry on a road-pavement in Fort. He attracted a large clientele by telling the crowd that he was the only man who had taken up Kovoor's challenge and succeeded. As proof, he exhibited a framed press photograph of himself signing the agreement before me, taken at my bungalow, and published in the "Savasa" four months ago.

To prevent him from perpetrating this fraud on innocent and ignorant public, I sent him a registered letter asking him to come and demonstrate his so-called powers on 15th October 1971. A copy of this letter was also hand-delivered to him. But he never came!

Mr. S. Sittampalam, the former commissioner of Inland Revenue, seems to have taken to the practice of fortune-telling through astrology in a big way after his retirement. Unlike the pavement fortune-teller who hoodwinks a few individuals, Mr. Sittampalam appears to be specialising in political predictions for the nation as a whole.

The publication of some of Mr. Sittampalam's astrological predictions about the country in an English Sunday newspaper provoked me to issue an open challenge to him to prove his fortune telling ability by facing a simple test in public.

Though numerous persons wrote supporting and opposing my challenge, Mr. Sittampalam, like all other occultists, never came forward to take up my challenge.

The Tamil newspaper "Thinakaran Varamanjari" published an article about a "Bhagawan" Neelakanda Babaji of Tamil Nadu in India, by one of his local devotees. This so-called Bhagawan was described as an incarnation of God—Avathar—capable of performing many miracles like "Bhagawan" Sathya Sai Baba, also of India. One paragraph in that article was as follows:—

"Among the many who have heard the fame and reputation of the Bhagawan and visited him to obtain blessings are, the Prime Minister Indira Gandhi, the former President Dr. S. Radhakrishnan and Maharaja of Mysore. The Bhagawan while blessing them materialised crystal 'Siva Lingam' in his hand from nowhere and gave it to these distinguished visitors. As a result they are still continuing to live in triumph and fame."

To check up the truth about this unbelievable story, I wrote to both the Prime Minister Indira Gandhi and Dr. Radhakrishnan. I was not at all shocked to receive the following reply from the Private Secretary to the Prime Minister of India.

"There is no truth in the story that the Prime Minister called on Neelakanda Babaji and he produced a lingam' from nowhere."

It is this type of false stories that make credulous people believe that saints, swamis, gurus, rishis, yogis, mystices, bhagawans, arahars, siddhas and gods have supernatural powers.

Recently a swamiji, who claimed to be from Rishikesh in Himalayas, said at a Bhajan meeting, and later at a press interview, that 'Kovoor' is an Avathar (incarnation of God) in search of truth! This crafty man might have made this preposterous statement just to placate the increasing number of youths in this country who see more reason and sense in rationalism than in religious beliefs based on absurdities.

This absurd statement of thc so-called holy man resulted in many credulous persons coming to my bungalow to have a 'darsan' and to obtain blessings from me. To undo the great harm done by this bluffer-swami Shantanand, I had to refute it through newspapers. Had I been an imposter like Sai Baba, Neelakanda Babaji and Pandrimalai Swamigal, it would have been, indeed, a grand opportunity for me to hoodwink thousands of gullibles and become fabulously rich!

On two occasions, after I spoke on "Magic, Miracles and Witchcraft" at public meetings in Colombo and Kalutara, I produced 'holy ash', Sai Baba-wise, by waving my out-stretched hands in air, just to convince the audience that the so-called materialisation of things from 'nowhere' by Bhagawans are only similar jugglery

The newspaper reports about my 'miracle' provoked a Sai Baba devotee to write to the Ceylon Daily News

"Only gullibles like Mr. Kovoor's followers would swallow what he so authoritatively states that production of holy ash by saints and swamis is mere magic and not a miracle."

He concluded his letter by "confirming that the production of holy ash by a saint is a miracle and not magic because he himself had the rare opportunity of witnessing a well-known spiritual personage producing it by mere wave of his hand in the presence of sceptic scientists."

In answer to this I challenged him and all other devotees of so-called Bhagawans to produce any one of them to materialise holy ash, lingam or any other object without resorting to trickery under fraud-proof conditions in my presence. I offered a reward of any amount above Rs. 1,000 and below Rs. 100,000 on a reciprocal basis if it is found that no trickery is involved.

Although nobody has taken up any of the numerous challenges of mine, I am, in a way happy that these challenges which are to remain open till my death, have helped numerous intelligent persons to realise that there is nothing supernatural in the universe. All that take place in nature are natural. There are no miracles, but only mysteries. Many of the mysteries of our forebears are solved today. Many of the mysteries of today may or may not be solved by tomorrow's scientists. Till that time it is absurd to give supernatural interpretations to unsolved mysteries!

## Chapter 2

### *GODMEN OF INDIA*

Although no God was responsible for the creation of the Universe and the living things in it, man on the planet earth was responsible for the creation of numerous gods in the past, and probably he will continue to do so in future.

Recently I happened to see a film at the Lionel Wendt Theatre, Colombo, about a 15-year old boy of India in the process of being made into a Godman by his crafty father, a few publicity agents and hundreds of neurotic devotees. This Godboy—Guru Maharaj Ji—who became notorious by being caught by the Indian Customs at Palam airport for smuggling undeclared foreign currency and traveller's cheques worth Rs. 4 lakhs, a necklace valued at Rs. 70,000 and wrist watches worth Rs. 1.5 lakhs, will Estill continue to attract thousands of mentally unbalanced hippies, flower girls and boys, who are constantly in search of mental stimulants be it be booster drugs or transcendental meditation.

#### HIGHLY TALENTED

This boy, who is highly talented in speech and action-even good enough to become a successful film star—taught to repeat parrot-like meaningless talks in a spiritual jargon by his crafty father, who himself earned a living, posing as a Godman before gullibles in north India. Like most Godmen of India, he too claims to have descended to the plains from 'the foothills of the Himalayas'.

Before that country became free, the Godmen of India earned their living in India itself by hoodwinking the credulous among the Indians by reclining their ash-smeared bodies on beds of nails, sitting cross-legged—topless and bottomless—in meditation, or by performing a few 'miracles' using conjuring tricks. But, after independence of India they have started seeking fresh pastures abroad, especially in Western countries where India has earned a false reputation for spirituality. For Europeans and Americans anyone from India in a flowing garb is an authority on matters spiritual.

## GARB OF HOLY MEN

Some of these Godmen who went to western countries made periodical returns to their home country with some of their European and American devotees. This encouraged more and more crafty men of India to go abroad in the garb of holy men taking new names as Gurus, Swamijis, Mahathmas, Anandas, Babas, Bhagawans, Rishis, Maharishis, Yogi Maharaj, etc.

Most of these Godmen succeeded beyond their expectations to amass wealth and to collect rich devotees round them. It has now become such a lucrative trade that the Godmen of India have become good foreign exchange earners for that country, so much so, that while it is very difficult for a genuine traveller to get an exit passport, there seems to be no difficulty for the Godmen of that country to go abroad. Godmen trade appears to be a state-patronised business of secular India!

## QUALIFICATION OF A GODMAN

Godman Maharishi Mahesh Yogi was more successful than the rest because he was fortunate in getting the millionaire pop-musicians—the Beatles—as his devotees. He even owned a private plane. Though there was a big set back in his divine trade when the Beatles left him because, according to Beatle John Lennon, "there was a big hallabaloo about the Maharishi attempting to rape one of their women—Mia Farrow", he still has a substantial following just as Guru Maharaj Ji has even after being caught as a smuggler.

What are the qualifications needed to become a successful Godman? First, he must be skilled in woolly talks using meaningless jargons such as self-liberation, self-realisation, self-purification, ultimate reality, cosmic force, cosmic intelligence, cosmic soul, cosmic mind, descarnate life, extra-cerebral mind, karmic force, nirvanic consciousness, divine force, divine light, extra-sensory perception, kundalini etc.

Secondly, he must be able to perform a few conjuring tricks under the pretext of 'miracles.'

## JUGGLING TRICKS

The third and the most important requisite is to have a few publicity agents to spread numerous cock-and-bull stories about the miraculous powers of the Godman through books, newspapers, films, radio and the TV.

With suitable publicity, devotees will gather round a godman just like flies round a decomposing carcass.

In 1972 during my visit to India for the filming of "Punarjanmam" and "Maru Piravi" based on one of my psychiatric cases, I had to attend a few receptions and press conferences at Madras, Bangalore, Calicut, Trichur, Ernakulam, Kottayam, Quilon and Trivandrum. Answering questions from pressmen I said that nobody in the world ever had or has at present divine or supernatural powers, and all the so-called miracles of Godmen are mere juggling tricks performed before gullibles who have neither the courage nor the commonsense to investigate.

To substantiate my statement I said that I would be prepared to pay an award of Rs. 100,000 to any Godman who can perform a miracle before me under fraud-proof conditions.

This challenge of mine which received wide publicity in India became a noose round the necks of Indian Godmen, and panicked thousands of their devotees. From that time I was inundated with letters from diverse types of religionists and Godmen saying that they could prove to me the existence of supernatural powers.

A few of them were foolhardy to publish through newspapers boasting articles about their divine powers: Dr. Vadlamudi through the "Decan Herald", C. St. Teerthankar through "The Hindu" and "The Times of Ceylon", R. P. Tiwari through the "Indian Express" and the "Bharat Jyoti", and an anonymous person from Kalna through the "Amrita Bazaar Patrika" said that they were prepared to take up my challenge.

In answer to all these claims made through letters and newspapers, I invited them to confirm their acceptance of my challenge by making an earnest deposit of Rs. 100 with a nominee of mine in Bombay and another in Bihar. On receipt of the deposit from any Godman my nominee would check up the genuineness of the claimant by conducting a preliminary test using one of the following simple tests: —

The contestant would be asked either to produce an exact replica of a one-rupee currency note shown to him, or to read the serial number of a currency note in my nominee's pocket sealed up in an envelope. If the Godman succeeds in either of the two tests, his deposit would be refunded. On hearing from my nominee about the success of a Godman, I would go to India to conduct my test in public under fraud-proof conditions, and pay the promised award of Rs. 1 lakh if he succeeds.

I insisted on the preliminary test and a refundable nominal deposit just to avoid being played out by the fraudulent claims of these charlatans.

## NO TAKERS

With the publication of these conditions in Indian and Sri Lanka newspapers ended the tall talks of these hoaxers. I am still waiting to see one taking my challenge by making the earnest deposit!

Conjuring tricks and the fictitious claims of Godmen and Godwomen like Sathya Sai Baba, Neelkanda Baba, Pandrimalai Swamigal, Acharya Rajanish, Vadlamudi, Teerthaker, Tiwari, Dattabal, Gurudev Mukthanand, Nirmala Devi, Triprayar Yogini, Poojya Dadaji, Swami Chinmayanda, Ananda Murthy, Guru Maharaj Ji and others will not become miraculous simply because a scientist like Dr. Bhagavantham or a Governor like K. K. Shah is prepared to believe them blindly without investigating.

A scientist who believes without verification is thoroughly unscientific. No real scientist will refrain from investigation fearing the sanctity of a person or an object.

## GULLIBLES AND FOOLS

At several public meetings I have 'materialised' holy ash by putting up my hands in the air. I was shocked to see several women wrapping the ash I gave in paper and putting it in their handbags. Like Dr. Bhagavantham and K. K. Shah, those credulous women thought that I 'materialised' the ash by my divine powers. Coming back to the stage I told them that the ash I gave was prepared by my wife by burning dry cow dung, and brought from Sri Lanka as I anticipated such a question in the land of Bhagawans! Had I been searched before the act, my cat would have been out of the bag. Sathya Sai Baba would never allow his body to be searched because he does not want to let his cat out!

He who does not allow his miracles to be investigated is a crook; he who does not have the courage to investigate a miracle is a gullible; and he who is prepared to believe without verification is a fool!

Can't the devotees of Godmen realise that their Bhagawans are as helpless as other human beings? Like all humans these so-called Godmen have hunger, they fall ill, and finally all of them die.

Some of the local devotees of Sathya Sai Baba found fault with me for writing about their godman undergoing a surgical operation for appendicitis. One doctor devotee had the audacity and credulity to say at a meeting of devotees, without any feeling of shame that it was not for removing his own appendix that the Bhagawan Sai Baba underwent surgical operation. "Out of compassion for a devotee whose appendix was giving him trouble, the Bhagawan took the diseased appendix into his own body in exchange for his healthy one, and it was that diseased appendix of the devotee that was removed from the Bhagawan's Body!"

## MATERIALISED IN AIRPLANE

It is a pity that there are gullible fools even among scientists prepared to believe this type of stories! One Bhagawan says he drove a car without petrol. Another fellow says he became a Godman after seeing a 6-ft. lingam grow out from a palmyrah fruit. One Bhagawan materialised in the cockpit of an American devotee's plane and saved it from crashing.

Another fellow claims that the waters of a river parted for him to drive a car across. One devotee claims that his hernia was cured after applying Baba's Holy ash.

Another devotee's hernia was cured by the Bhagawan operating on him without surgical instruments. Thus goes the long list of Godmen's miracles.

Why do people fall easy prey to these charlatan cultures? The answer is mass hysteria. When two or three persons genuflex or prostrate before a Godman, the others will simply follow. These imitators lack independent thinking and reasoning. If some one shouts "Haro hara" "halleluyah" or "Sadh Sadh" they too will shout.

While the imaginary gods like Jehovah, Allah, Brahma, Vishnu, Siva, etc., do not exist, Godmen do exist, and are a menace to humanity.

## Chapter 3

# *DR. BHAGAVANTHAM AND SATHYA SAI BABA*

During my visit to Madras in 1972 to appear in my own role in the film "Punarjanman", I was invited to give a lecture at the Indian Institute of Technology at Gulndy. During a conversation before the lecture one of the professors at the institute told me that the majority of youths who take to the study of science and technology do so not because they have any scientific attitude or aptitude, but just because such a course helps them to get lucrative jobs. The reason why some of the eminent scientists of India have given up their science, and become "devotees" of Godmen of that country was because they have found that they can make more money by being in collusive devotion to such hoaxers than by continuing scientific pursuits.

A few months ago the editor of a mass-circulating weekly of India wrote me a letter saying that the Editorial Board of his weekly has decided to publish a symposium on "SATHYA SAI BABA—IS HE AN INCARNATION OF GOD OR A CHARLATAN?", and wanted me to be the first contributor to the series.

My article was serialised in three issues. It was then followed by two articles countering my thesis by Dr. S. Bhagavantham, M.Sc., D.Sc., Ph.D., a former scientific adviser to the Government of India.

Dr. Bhagavantham started his article by saying that in his youth he was a rationalist like me, but after witnessing some of the 'miracles' of Bhagawan Sathya Sai Baba, he had to give up his rationalism!

He then continued to describe numerous 'miracles' said to have been performed by Sathya Sai Baba at various times in various places. There was absolutely no mention in the two articles of any one having conducted investigations to establish that they were all genuine miracles, and not conjurer's tricks. The two articles appeared to be clear examples of how unscientific even a good scientist can become if he is a victim of religio-maniacal neurosis or avarise for lucre!

In the whole lot of the miracle stories mentioned by Dr. Bhagavantham, there was only one that was amenable to investigation. I quote below that story:—

"The wonderful experience, some years ago, of a world-famous "watch manufacturer of Japan, while he was on tour in India, was awe-inspiring.

"After completing the Seiko series of watches he made the model of a more superior type, and kept it in his safe for further tests.

"While touring in India he paid a visit to Sathya Sai Baba's abode just out of curiosity. On seeing the Japanese gentleman among the devotees Sathya Sai Baba materialised a small parcel from the air and gave him. On opening the parcel he was astonished to see the same watch that was kept in his safe. When he saw along with the watch the silk ribbon and the label with the new name of the watch and its price marked on it, all his doubts about the divine powers of Sathya Sai Baba simply melted away. He fell prostrate at Sathya Sai Baba's feet and worshipped him. Since then he is an ardent devotee of the Bhagawan.

"On his return to Japan, he was shocked to see that the watch he had kept in his safe was not there. What his Personal Secretary told him was still more startling. The Secretary said that a divine-looking person with bushy hair walked into the office one day, opened the safe and walked away with the watch."

Does Dr. Bhagavantham, who is the holder of covetable qualifications in science, think that a thesis of this nature to prove the miraculous powers of a man, by any scientist, will be accepted by an academic body of scientists if it is not backed by scientific investigations and fool-proof evidence ?

Although Dr. Bhagavantham is reluctant to test the veracity of his Godman's miraculous powers, I decided to do it myself. With this aim in view I wrote the following letter to Dr. Bhagavantham:—

"Tiruwalla", Panankada Lane,
Colombo-6, Sept. 11, 1973

"Dear Dr. Bhagavantham,

I read your story about a Japanese watch manufacturer getting his own watch that was kept in a safe in Japan, materialised in India from air by Sathya Sai Baba.

My scientific attitude does not permit me to accept this fantastic story as true without verification. My doubt is enhanced by the reported statement of his personal Secretary. The first reaction of a responsible Secretary when a stranger walks into the office and opens the safe, would be to raise the alarm and to summon the police.

As I feel it is unscientific even for a scientist to believe this type of cock-and-bull story without verification, I request you to kindly let me know the name and address of this Japanese so that I may verify the truth about it.

Your failure to help me to conduct this investigation by withholding this information, will lead me to suspect your sincerity and honesty, and discard all what you have said about Sathya Sai Baba as utter falsehood deliberately propagated with ulterior motive and vested interest.

Yours in search of Truth,
Abraham T. Kovoor"

As there was no response from Dr. Bhagavantham even after two months, I decided to pursue the matter on my own. The Japanese Embassy in Sri Lanka was kind enough to provide me with the name and address of the proprietor of the Seiko watch manufacturing firm.

In my letter dated 30th October, 1973 to Mr. Shoji Hattori, president of K. Hattori & Co. Ltd., the manufacturers of Seiko watches, I reproduced Dr. Bhagavantham's story about the miracle, and requested him to provide me with answers to the following questions: —

1. Did you or any other partner of yours visit Sathya Sai Baba of India any time?

2. Did Sai Baba materialise a watch from air and present it to you or to any of your partners?
3. Did your personal Secretary tell you or any of your partners that a stranger opened the safe and walked away with a watch?
4. Are you or any of your partners a devotee of Sai Baba?

For the benefit of numerous innocent devotees of Godmen of India I reproduce below Mr. Hattori's reply. This I do with the sincere hope that they will be sensible enough to realise the truth that these charlatans who go about in the garb of holy men have numerous agents like Dr. Bhagavantham everywhere working in collusion to propagate the huge hoax and profit materially.

SEIKO

K. HATTORI & CO., LTD.
5, Koyobashi 2-chome,
chuo-ku,
Tokyo 104.
Established 1881
Cable: Hattori Tokyo.
Phone: Tokyo 563-2111.
November 8, 1973.

Dr. A. T. Kovoor,
Pamankada Lane,
Colombo-6, Sri Lanka.

Dear Dr. Kovoor,

Thank you for your letter of October 30th. I can appreciate your interest in conducting scientific research of paranormal claims, but I am in no way able to further your knowledge as regards the man mentioned in your letter, Mr. Sai Baba. Neither I nor any members of my staff have ever made the acquaintance of this individual. I am sure that these reports are completely unfounded I must therefore reply in the negative to all four of your questions concerning this incident.

Sincerely yours,
K. HATTORI & CO., LTD.
Sgd. Shoji Hattori,
President

On receipt of this letter I wrote the following letter to Dr. Bhagavantham enclosing a photostat copy of Mr. Shoji Hattori's letter.

"

Dear Dr Bhagavantham,

Absence of any response from you to my request made over two months ago has made me suspect the veracity of your story about the Japanese watch manufacturer getting his own watch that was kept in his safe in Japan, from Sai Baba. To pursue my investigation in the matter, I got the name and address of Seiko watch manufacturer from the Japanese Embassy in Sri Lanka.

In his reply to my enquiry, Mr. Shoji Hattori, President of K. Hattori & Co., Ltd., who are the manufacturers and proprietors of Seiko watches writes:—

"I can appreciate your interest in conducting scientific research of paranormal claims, but I am in no way able to further your knowledge as regards the man mentioned in your letter, Mr. Sai Baba. Neither I nor any members of my staff have ever made the acquaintance of this individual. I am sure that these reports are completely unfounded

If Mr. Shoji Hattori is not the person concerned in your story, please let me know about it, and provide me with the correct name and address. Absence of any reply from you for this letter also, will only confirm my firm belief that you are an agent of Sathya Sai Baba doing propaganda for him with ulterior motive and vested interest.

Yours in search of Truth,
Abraham T. Kovoor".

Since there was no reply so far to this letter also, I had to confirm my belief that Dr. Bhagavantham is in collusion with the charlatan Sathya Sai Baba to do false propaganda for him with ulterior motive and vested interest.

## Chapter 4

### *THE CONCEPT OF GOD*

I wish to express my views on this burning question which is becoming more and more controversial as the horizon of human knowledge is expanding.

The renowned palaeontologist and Roman Catholic priest Teilhard de Chardin, in his book "The Phenomenon of Man" opines that the emergence of man on earth is the culmination of organic evolution guided by an all powerful supreme intelligence, which he prefers to call God.

The former Bishop of Woolwich Dr. Robinson, a liberal theologian of modern times who has discarded the anthropomorphic God from his heavenly abode, speaks in his book "Honest to God" about an impersonal intelligent God which he says is in, and full control of everything in nature.

Nearer home Rev. Fred de Silva of the Methodist church in a Pamplet entitled "Does Science leave room for God" says "The various branches of science and knowledge reflect different aspects of god. The mystery of god is partially revealed in Physics, partly in Chemistry, partly in Botany, Zoology, Physiology and so on, the artists and the poets also reveal the same aspects of god. True religion combines all these aspects and adds a spiritual dimension to it all. What keeps the moon in a fixed orbit is the co-ordination of the gravitational pulls of the sun, earth and the moon. Is this co-ordination a matter of chance? I find it more reasonable to believe there is an intelligence behind these co-ordinate happenings. I give the name of god to that supreme intelligence."

Let us now consider what this impersonal intelligence these liberal theologians are speaking of. Intelligence, a mental attribute cannot exist without the functioning of a brain tissue. Bionics, the new branch of science explore the electronic behaviour of the physiological and mental activities of organisms.

There cannot be a mind or intelligence without life and body and there cannot be life without a body. Just as there cannot be fire without a fuel to burn, there cannot be life without a body conducting respiration. Thus to speak about impersonal intelligence is crazy nonsense.

Life is not the same thing as mind. A potato or a disembodied heart can continue to live under favourable conditions, but they cannot have minds because they have no brain tissues. What is this spiritual dimension Rev. de Silva speaks of? This usage has come down from the unfounded conception that all living organisms have immortal souls or spirits in their bodies. Spiritualists believe that a discarnate soul has both life and mind. This is an absurd belief because it is impossible to have life and mind without a respiring body. These bodyless 'spirits' are said to materialise, fully clad of course, before neurotic visionaries. How this disembodied spirits can speak without lungs and vocal cord, or how they can do physical acts without muscular bodies, or from where do they get their dresses to be fully clad, do not seem to bother these blind believers in spirits.

If dead persons leave behind their 'spirits' to haunt the places of their death, the moon might become a haunted place before long because there is nothing to prevent one or more astronauts or cosmonauts meeting with their death on it in future. If such a calamity occurs, the Americans ami Russians will have to recruit a few kattadiyas from Ceylon to be taken to the moon to conduct an exercising thovil there, so that the place may be made safe for future moonlandings!

We have to accept the scientific fact that everything in the universe is material. The old distinction between matter and energy, matter and mind, material and spiritual, no longer exist in the light of modern science. The fundamental particles that constitute matter are nothing but energy. Thus, the 'mind over matter' concept of philosophers is now an out-moded one. Mind is purely material in origin and working.

The renowned neurologist Walter Hess, who was awarded the Nobel Prize for his marvellous discoveries about the working of the mind has proved the material nature of the so-called spiritual values or spiritual attributes such as love, compassion, kindness, metta, muditha, karuna etc. He has demonstrated that mental emotions such as love, friendship, hatred, compassion, cruelty, kindness, anger, hunger, amor, sympathy, apathy, pain, pleasure, desires, dislikes, fear etc., could be induced at will by stimulating the respective brain centre with electrical impulse. Thus Walter Hess proved that the so-called spiritual values are nothing but electro-chemical activities of the neurons, and not divinely inspired.

Since the universe is material, and matter can neither be created nor be destroyed, the question of a personal or impersonal creator does not arise. Like all chemical changes, all what is wanted for the chemical evolution of living matter from inter matter, are suitable conditions or environments, and not a super-intelligent creator.

Truly to answer these liberal theologians is not an easy task. Ofcourse, one could answer them with an impossible counter question. Where did this god come from? Let us examine where the evidence, reason and logic may lead.

First of all let us look at the world about us, then at the planets and satellites of our own solar system, and then at the galaxies and the quasars. Looking out into the universe in all directions, the astronomer sees countless stars similar to our own sun, and has estimated that their number exceeds one-hundred-thousand-million-billion, an inconceivable number scattered at inconceivable distances from us. Since all stars are evolving, we can see them as they were hundred years, and many hundreds of thousand years ago.

The observable universe has a radius of one billion light years. This is not the entire universe, but only as much as may be seen through the world's largest telescope. The unseen portion of the universe which contains many more galaxies has been discovered by radio telescopes which pick up the rays that are emitted from them.

Within the observable universe, it is estimated that there are no less than one-hundred-million galaxies, some of which are larger than our own milky way galaxy, to which the solar system belongs as a minute speck. All these galaxies appear to be receding from each other at an ever increasing speed.

It is estimated that there are at least one million planetary systems in the milky way galaxy alone. The planets in these systems possess the same elements as our earth. If similar conditions exist, there is no reason to reject the idea that, with the chemico-electric basis for the beginning of life on earth, millions of these planets are inhabited with beings more or less like those on this earth.

With the continual breaking down and re-formation of the elements in these gigantic conglomerations of matter, we may well speculate as to whether there may be a great engineer who designed and produced the materials of the total universe. The only answer is NO.

Or we may ask: Is there any purpose in nature? From our observation of nature we can derive no adequate basis for such a belief. On this minute speck we can call earth in nature and upon which we dwell, events happen such as the magnific ent growth of our forest trees. This growth over centuries of time evolved from simple algae. Nourished by the solar energy they attained their present state after many years, and then along comes one of those destructive forces of nature—a tornado—which is also caused by the sun's energy and this destructive eliminates all the trees of that beautiful forest. Again we ask: was there any plan or purpose in that destructive action of the tornado? The answer again must be NO. The conditions are such that both events were the result that were possible under those conditions.

During the past two million years man evolved from a wild animal stage, hunting for his food with a club or a pointed stick, to an intelligent being capable of visiting the moon, worshipped as a god by his forebears, and probably before long other neighbouring gods like Mars, Jupiter, Saturn, retains many of the characteristics of animal and the barbarian from whom he evolved.

Since the scientist has accurately determined the age of the oldest rock discovered as 3 billion years, the age of the earth should be over 3 billion years—perhaps 4.5 billion. Comparison to this with the biblical era of creation 5975 years ago, we see that it is less than one-two million part of the geological age of our own planet.

We all marvel at the wonders and beauty of things in nature. But let us look around us at all things and see the good as well as the bad in nature. If there is a creator, all things both beautiful and ugly, good and bad, must come from him. And why has a benevolent god created so many evil things? If everything that happens in the universe is pre-ordained by god, then this mysterious being should take full responsibility for all the miseries, murders, torturing, wars, genocides, famines, plagues, rapes, robberies, and all types of vices. But no: religions have always had to have it both ways, while god was omnipotent, man was also responsible. He had free will, and so was accountable for his evil thoughts and actions. Should not the blame fall on the ominiscient creator who gave man free will to be evil?

If the wife of a person who escapes death in an air-crash, as he was late to arrive at the airport, should thank god for saving his life, should not the wives and husbands of all those who died in the crash curse the god for causing their death? If there is a creator god he cannot escape the responsibility of killing thousands of Bang la Desh refugees by cholera bacteria he himself created.

We marvel at the wonder of the human eye picking up an image of a thing, and the nerve that carries this image to the brain so that we realise the true picture exactly, and think that all these must be the work of an intelligent creator interested in the welfare of man. But, let us also look at the deadly fangs of a cobra, delicately fashioned as a doctor's hypodermic needle, hollow and sharp, provided with a deadly poisonous gland with strong muscles to inject the poison into the helpless victim. Think of the thousands who die yearly due to cyclones, tornados, earth-quakes and volcanic erruptions. If these be the work of a creator, should he not take the responsibility for the death of numerous innocent men. women and children by these natural catastrophies?

Is Teilhard de Chardin right in thinking that evolution is guided by an all-intelligent, omnipotent power? Organic evolution, like all evolutions in nature, is a blind process producing both fit and misfit organisms depending on diverse genetic and environmental factors. The misfits perish and the fit survive in the prolonged struggle for existence. The fossil history of our earth shows that more organisms have become extinct than surviving ones. Thus it is clear that evolution is a process of trial and error, and creation by trial and error cannot be the way of an omnipotent and omniscient god. To say that organic evolution is guided intelligently by an unseen power is utter nonsense.

Some of the modern liberal theologians try to prove that the Biblical story of creation is compatible with the modern theory of evolution by saying that one day of god is equivalent to millions of years of man. They forget the funny situation of poor Adam having to wait for millions of years to get his wife Eve, because she was not created on the same day with Adam. Also, since there was morning and evening every day of creation, our earth which takes only 24 hours to complete one rotation, should have taken millions of years to do so during the Genesis days.

Teilhard de Chardin opines that man is the final goal of god's creation, the omega point of organic evolution. His concept of the universe seems to be not only theocentric, but also geocentric and homocentric; Father Chardin though an eminent palaeontologist, could not get over the Catholic belief implanted in his mind from his childhood, that god created man in his own image, and everything in the universe for his benefit

If man emerged on this planet as the culmination of all creations, it follows that there will be no more evolution in nature. It is absurd to think that the universe had reached the end of its evolution with the emergence of man on earth in the image of the creator himself. Is the earth so important a planet in the whole universe for the so-called creator to put his special creation—the god-like man on it?

When one looks at the immensity of the universe, in comparison to which our earth is less than a minute particle of dust, surely an intelligent power that could create such an immensity would have little interest in the earth—let alone the man on it. Why should an omniscient god create a vast universe for man when he cannot see even a billionth part of it? It just does not make sense.

By his advanced knowledge in medical science man is defeating and defying god every day, enabling millions of misfits to survive god-ordained death, and continue to procreate more and more misfits. To make up for this damaging effect, man is now tampering with nature, or shall I say, to breed better human beings and domesticated animals and plants by the application of genetic engineering and selective breeding. Artificial insemination, test-tube babies, cryogenic prolongation of life, extra-uterine conception etc., are new techniques unknown to god.

Whether religionists like it or not, the time is not far off when a Minister holding the portfolio of human breeding will be deciding who and who can be licenced to procreate children. While even the misfits will have the freedom to enjoy sex in a future permissive society, they will not have the freedom to have children unless they obtain special licences from the Ministry of Human Breeding.

Does god exist? There is absolutely no evidence to establish that God or Gods exist

## Chapter 5

## *IS THERE A LIFE AFTER DEATH ?*

I do not hold the view that my life is located in a particular spot in my body. Life is generated in all living cells in my body, and is sustained by the oxidatory chemical action which goes on in them. This chemical action is maintained by my breathing and blood-circulation. It is not in any way different from the production of heat and light energies during combustion of the hydrocarbon in a burning candle. Heat and light do not depart from a burning candle when it is put out, and return to it when relit.

It is just a case of cessation of chemical activity and production of energy. Similarly there is nothing to get out from my body when it dies as a result of termination of breathing and blood-circulation. If by any change my dead body is resuscitated by some of the modern techniques, it will be wrong to think that the 'departed life or soul' re-entered the survived body.

My death will not be taking place abruptly at a particular moment in time. I began to die some 70 years ago. I started my life as a parasite on my mother. About one-eighth of my body died in the form of the umbilical cord and placenta on the day I terminated my parasitic mode of life. From that day onward I have been dying as well as growing. While numerous cells in my body died daily, numerous new ones were born. Large quantities of dead tissues have escaped my body by way of cropped and shaved hair, peeled off skin, cut nails, dropped teeth, and the millions of internal cells discarded as waste during urination and perspiration.

Accidental cuts and bruises, bacterial and virus infections, physical and mental work> exposure to ultra-violet and infra-red rays of sun, action of caustic and corrosive chemicals I have come in contact with while working in science laboratories, consumption of highly spiced pungent curries etc., have been responsible for killing major parts of my seventy-year old body.

Once a part of my body was removed by surgical operation. Forty years ago a minute cell separated from my body, merged with a foreign cell, and continued to grow out of my body. It is still growing and proliferating in Paris as Dr. Aries Kovoor.

During my youth the rate of birth of new cells in my body was far greater than the rate of death. Hence, I began to grow and put on weight, reaching a maximum of 185 pounds in my 40th year. I maintained this maximum weight for a few years more when the rate of birth and death of cells in the body was equal Thereafter the rate ot death steadily kept ahead of birth, so much so, that my present weight is only 125 pounds. The total weight of the dead tissues which have escaped my body, all these years would amount to lakhs of pounds. This process of continued death will go on till the day when there will be no more cells left behind to multiply. Even after the death of all the cells in my body, the cornea of my eyes will continue to live in the eyes of a lucky stranger.

The death of the 125 pounds of my present body will be a major event in my life of continued birth and death, because my brain—the seat of my mind—would cease to function, bringing to an end, my individuality and age.

My last breath will not be in any way different from the present one. Then, as well as now. I shall be breathing out carbon dioxide and water vapour.

I do not believe that I have a soul or spirit to survive my death, and go to heaven or hell, or to roam about as my ghost, or even to be reborn.

If at all there is a soul, the major part of it should have escaped from me long ago with large mass of dead tissues which have left me already and even after the death of the present 125 pounds of tissues, a fraction of that soul should remain in the body of the stranger who would be receiving the corneal graft.

I am an individual because, as a highlv evolved animal, I have a set of centralised nervous, respiratory, circulatory and alimentary svstems. But during the earlv stage of my development in my mother's womb, before the centralised biological functions started, I too had a dividual stage like many lower animals and most plants. While I was in my mother's womb, had the foetal tissue or the fertilized egg divided and separated into two or three parts, I would Irave had one or two identical (cogenital) brothers born with me sharing fractions of my original soul or reborn personality.

Though sound and logical, these postulations will be rejected by people who are indoctrinated or brainwashed about souls and re-births, because these are not in line with the teachings of 'religions'. •

Thus, though all religious teachings 'postulate a life after death', I have not any valid reason or evidence to believe it.

On 7th June, during question time after a lecture I delivered at Wesley College, a teacher from the audience asked me what I thought about the doctrine of rebirth. At my request one of the prefects brought a cigar box from my car containing the headless body of a praying mantis. On 22nd May I decapitated a praying mantis to be used for demonstration at a talk on rebirth I was to give next day. .

Sixteen days later, on opening the box, the headless insect started to hop about. If rebirth is an objective reality, the severed head which died 16 days earlier, because it could not breathe, should have been reborn somewhere, while the body which continued to breathe and live, will have to be reborn somewhere else when it dies of starvation a few days later! A case of one organism re-incarnating in two places!

One Mr. Sena says there is difference between cellular life and 'the other life' which he calls 'essence of life or eternal life'. This eternal life, he says, "is believed to traverse time and space until it finally reaches a state when it should be no more"

I fail to understand how a life which "would be no more" can be called 'eternal life' Utter nonsense. Life, whether it is produced in a single cell, or in all the cells of a multicellular organism, is the same. There is absolutely no difference between the life in a plant, a worm or man. The difference is in the degree of the mental development, and not in life. The quality of the mind varies according to the evolution of the nervous system. While there is no mind in a live potato, there is a rudimentary mind in a worm, and a highly developed mind in man. We have no reason to believe that man is the most intelligent organism in the universe.

The headless praying mantis could not only continue to produce life, but also had a rudimentary mind because it had numerous ganglia in the body. Instead of one, had I kept in the box two headless bodies, one of a male and another of a female, they would have mated, and the female body would have laid eggs and these eggs would have hatched out producing young mantises complete with heads! They could perform the conscious act of mating because they have mental faculties, though very rudimentary.

One Mr. Weeraratne says, “The breeding of primitive form of life by a sexual process do not come into the picture of rebirth.” What scientific evidence has he to make this statement? He continues, “Rebirth takes place at a higher level of evolution when the mind factor comes into operation”.

Probably this gentleman is not aware of the fact that an organism like a coelenterate, which has a nervous system, and therefore at least rudimentary mind, can be cut into several fragments, and each fragment can live and grow into coelenterates. Will these regenerated coelenterates have only fractions of the “reborn being” in the parent body? Even in the case of human beings, if the fertilised egg-cell after the ‘entry of the reborn being’ breaks up into four and are born as identical quadruplets, will those babies have only a quarter of the ‘reborn being’ in the zygote? How absurd

One Mr. Liyanage tries to prove rebirth through child prodigies and cogenital variations.

Explanations for cogenital variations are better sought in genetics and heredity than in karma and rebirth. Man has succeeded in producing prodigies among domesticated animals by selective breeding. The prodigious egg-layers like the ‘High Line’ hens, and the prodigious milk-yielders like the Cape cows are the products of selective breeding using man’s knowledge in the science of genetics and heredity. The prodigious characteristics of these animals are governed by their genes and DNA molecules, and not by their karma!

Time will not be far when man will be using his advanced knowledge in genetics to improve the qualities of his own species. I visualise a future when governments, discarding taboos, will be interfering with the freedom of the individual in the field of procreation. By this I do not mean that individuals with inferior or undesirable qualities will be deprived of their freedom to satisfy their sexual needs by legitimate means. Governments might take measures that such persons do not procreate.

Human procreation may become one of the most important national concerns needing guidance and control by expert geneticists and far-sighted statesmen. It may be that married couples will have to obtain special licence from the 'Ministry of Procreation' to have children.

Semen banks, like blood banks, may be established throughout the country for preserving specially selected semen for artificially inseminating specially selected women possessing desired qualities. Thus, when man adopts selective breeding for his own species, it will be possible to plan the birth of more and more human prodigies than at present. Today such prodigies are few and far between being the product of mere chance.

"Since the majority of the people of Sri Lanka believe in rebirth" will our Government think that it is necessary to instruct the Agricultural and Veternity Research Institute to improve the strain of cultivated plants and domesticated animals by selecting, the sires and dames for breeding according to their past karma, instead of the normal method of depending on cogenital factors?

To say that child prodigies are born with the memory of the acquired knowledge of the previous birth is as absurd as the assertion of some rebirth investigators like Prof. Ian Stevenson, Prof. H. N. Bannerji and Mr. V. F. Gunaratne that physical characteristics such as facial features, complexion, wounds and scars can re-appear in the reborn bodies. If it is true, it will be a death-blow to the Eye Donation Society. Fear of being reborn blind will prevent people from donating their eyes.

If the claim that mathematical prodigies can retain their knowledge in their reborn life is true, we can look forward to the wonderful day when a donkey, a mathematical prodigy in its previous life occupying the chair for mathematics at the University of Sri Lanka.

Stories about children recalling the memories of their previous lives have to be discarded as pure myths. All those who have investigated such cases dispassionately and scientifically have been able to discover the fictitious nature, and the fraud behind such stories.

The well-known American researcher into the field of Psychic phenomena Sprague de Camp, in his book "SPIRITS, STARS AND SPELLS" debunks the fraud behind the often cited Bridey Murphy and Simandini cases as authentic examples of proving rebirth through hypnotic regression (Pp. 246-249).

Mr. Liyanage, without adequate knowledge of biology, says, "The example of the death and resurrection of Peter Sellers quoted by Mr. Kovoor is puerile. For, if the brain had stopped getting its oxygen supply, no electronic pace-maker would have resurrected the man."

This gentleman holds the foolish view that live brain is a pre-requisite for resurrection or sustenance of life. What has the brain to do with the life in a bacterium, an egg, a potato, a zygote in the womb or a tissue in culture? Using the new technique of cryogenics it is possible to deep-freeze bodies before or immediately after death, and stored in cold chambers to be revived even after one or more centuries, is it the 'departed' life of the person that comes back from another 'reborn organism' to re-enter its old body? Do the brains of the frozen bodies remain alive for centuries? How silly!

These believers in rebirth fallaciously argue that the last thought of the dying man 'links up' with the next life. To substantiate this argument they cite the natural law governing the conservation of matter and energy.

To say that thoughts can survive the death of the thinker is as absurd as saying that a man's life continues to exist in a clock he happened to wind just before his death or that his thoughts continue to exist in a magnetic tape containing the record of his death-bed talks, or that a chicken continues to live in his body because he ate it.

If minds can have extra-cerebral existence capable of being reborn again and again, where were these minds before life originated on our planet? Can there be thought without a thinker, memory without a person to remember, or consciousness without someone to be conscious?

Just as there cannot be fire without fuel, there cannot be life and mind without a body and nervous tissue to produce them. Death is the termination of life.

The so-called soul is a combination of both life and mind. Since life and mind cannot survive the body, it is meaningless to talk about "an everlasting life", or an immortal soul. Goutama knew this truth, and preached the doctrine of 'anathma' more than twenty five centuries ago.

It is unfortunate that the doctrine of re-incarnation, a Brahminical belief which militates against 'anathma' doctrine crept into some Buddhist Scriptures long after the death of Goutama, the Buddha.

## Chapter 6

# *ASTROLOGY*

Astrology was known to man from primitive times, even before he gained any sound knowledge of Astronomy. Based on the positions of the sun; the moon, and the planets in the sky at the time a person is born, astrologers attempted to predict all the important events in the life of that person. History records that man has dabbled in astrology for more than five thousand years when his knowledge of the universe was crude and scrappy.

Belief in astrology stems from the foolish belief that human destinies as well as the movements of the heavenly bodies were controlled by a supreme being. Astrology was an attempt on the part of the primitive man to ascertain the intentions of the supreme being by studying the movements of the heavenly bodies he himself was controlling.

The fact. that many of the natural catastrophies such as cyclones,thunderstorms, tidal waves, gales, tornadoes, meteoric showers etc., result from forces outside the earth. made man falsely believe that his destinies also were guided by the sun, the moon, the planets and the stars outside the earth. The influence of the apparent posi--tions of the sun, to the weather and climate as well as the relationship between the phases of the moon and the tides, have helped him to confirm the wrong concception.

The early observers eagerly recorded the relative posi--tions of the sun, the moon and the visible planets, against the fixed stars of the zodiacal constellations whenever important events affecting the country and its king occurred. Every time such planetary positions repeated, they predicted similar events. If, for instance, there was a rainbow or an eclipse, or a comet in the sky when an enemy is defeated in a war, rainbows. eclipses and comets became good portents or omens. Similarly any occurrence in the sky during calamity, was regarded as an inauspicious portent. Thus the relative positions of the sun, the moon and visible planets became auspicious or inauspicious according to the good and bad events that occurred, when such positions were first observed.

At first astrology was consulted only to predict the affairs of the king. It was considered that the welfare of the common man depended on the fortunes and mis fortunes of their country and their king.

Astrology flourished even before 3000 B.C., in countries like Mesapotamia, Babylon, Chaldea, China and India. It was from Babylon that astrology spread into countries like Assyria, Greece, Egypt and Rome in the west and from India it spread into the neighbouring countries including Ceylon. The earliest known book in Astrology 'Tetrabiblious' was written by Claudeus Ptolomeus of Egypt. The Sanskrit 'Hora Sastra' of India is of unknown date and unknown author.

During the pre-Christian era, preparation of almanacs and astrological horoscopes were the monopoly of priests. Practice of astrology was a much more respected proffession than any other. Gradually astrology got separated from religion in China and the Islamic and Christian countries of west. This was mainly due to the teachings of Confucious, Prophet Mohammed and Jesus Christ. The teachings of Gauthama Buddha did not succeed in getting rid of astrology from Hindu India. Even Buddhism itself did not last long in India due to Brahminical opposition. Though Buddhism has become a major religion in Ceylon, astrology still flourishes among Buddhists in Ceylon, mainly due to Hindu influence. Ceylon is unique in the fact that it is the only country in the world which did create a chair for astrology in one of its state universities.

In India the bond between astrology and religions is maintained without a break for the last 5000 years. This is because of the fact that all the religious ceremonies of the Hindus have to be conducted during auspicious times, based on astrological calculations.

Just as alchemy was the forerunner of chemistry, and witchcraft the forerunner of medical science. astrology can proudly-claim to be the forerunner of modern astronomy. Even as back as 3000 B. C. astrologers were competent to prepare almanacs. This ability they achieved purely by naked-eye observations, without the aid of telescopes. There are historical evidences of star charts prepared by astrologists-astronomers of old. By the study of such charts they found that planetary incidents repeated once in 18 years and 11 and 13 days. Babylonians called this period as the SAROS cycle. Based on this Saros cycle astrologist-astronomers were able to prepare their almanacs and make astrological predictions.

Since comets were not subject to Saros cycle, astrologers were not able to predict the appearance of comets, although they attached great portents to their appearance. Even today astrologers consider comets as signs of imminent tragedies. Astronomers, on the other hand, have succeeded in calculating the time-cycle of many comets.

Just as the study of chemistry and medicine have helped scientists to discard alchemy and witchcraft, the study of astronomy has helped scientists to discard astrology as a pseudoscience. Before the 16th century most of the astronomers were believers in astrology. Till this time the Ptolomean concept that the earth was the centre of the universe was firmly held. The heliocentric nature of the solar system, first pronounced by Copernicus in the 16th century gave a shattering blow to astrology. Belief in astrology died out among astronomers in the 17th century when Newton's gravitational theory was accepted. But as the saying goes, "the cat has nine lives," superstitions have, not nine, but ninety nine lives.

Astrologers of today bolster up their case often quoting the names of Kepler, Galileo and Newton as astronomers of old, who believed in their cult. Of course, had Johannes Kepler continued his astrological practice instead of continuing his study of astronomy, he would not have died a penniless person. It is true that Galileo drew up a horoscope for the grand Duke Ferdinand of Tuscany. Galileo predicted for him, a long life, though he died a few weeks later. As for Newton, there is not a trace of evidence either in any of his books or in any of his letters indicating that he showed the slightest interest in astrology. I wish to mention Voltaire in this connection. He was the victim of two astrologers who predicted his death at the age of 32. He lived to be 84.

It is an incontrovertible fact that after the discovery of Kepler's laws, and Newtons explaining the movements of planets round the sun, not a single astronomer of repute has defended the stupidities of astrology. As the great astronomer Flamerian stated so admirably: “No fact of observation proves that planets and stars have any influence on our destinies”

The data on which astrologers base their predictions are utterly wrong and unscientific. It is absurd to attach any scientific value to conclusions arrived from wrong data. Their calculations are still based on the outmoded geocentric conception. For them, the sun and the moon are still planets. They do not know that the twelve houses of the zodiac have no objective reality. The zodiacal constellations are just arbitrary divisions of the sky. The constellations of stars and the relative positions of the planets are merely subjective configurations based on the optical perspective, depending on the position of the observer, if he happens to be, up in space in a space craft. It is impossible for an astrologer to prepare an astrological chart for a child born to a woman astronaut while she is in space orbit.

In reality there is nowhere in nature a constellation known as Aries, or a Taurus. Moreover, the first point of Aries is still reckoned by astrologers as the spring equinox, although on account of the astronomical phenomenon known as the ‘Precision of Equinoxes’ all the zodiacal constellations or houses no longer correspond with the constellations, after which they were named ages ago.

Planets Neptune, Uranus and Pluto do not find places in the data and charts of astrologers. These planets were not known to the originators of astrology. On the other hand they have two imaginary planets known as Rahu and Kethu in their charts. The primitive idea was that Rahu and Kethu were two heavenly serpents, who, on special dates, try to swallow the sun and the moon causing the solar and lunar eclipses. When later astrologers found that this was untenable they said that Rahu and Kethu were dark planets invisible to man, although he was subject to the influences of these unseen planets. In reality they are only the imaginary spots or nodes in space, where the apparent—not real—paths of the moon and the sun appear or intersect for an observer on the earth. Since Rahu and Kethu are not objective entities, it is absurd on the part of the astrologers to say that they have influence on the destinies of mankind.

Since the sun is millions and millions of miles away from the moon, there cannot be a Rahu or Kethu for an astronaut in space outside the orbit of the moon, because the sun and the moon do not intersect as far as he is concerned. Can there be an objective node in space, when a CTB bus on Galle road is intersected by a jumbo jet in the sky?

Astrologers who claim that every second makes a difference in the correctness of the horoscope reading, fail to make the necessary correction for light-time relativity, as astronomers do.

The authors of ancient books on astrology did not even know that the sun is a star and not a planet, that the radiant energy from heavenly bodies takes time to travel in space, that the moon is not a planet, and the positions of stars and planets one sees in the zodiacal constellations, when a child is born on earth, are only virtual and not real. They did not know that there is not a single star in the 12 zodiacal constellations which from the basis of astrological calculations, whose energies reach the earth in less than 4½ years. They did not know that many of the stars in the zodiacal signs are billions of light years away from earth. They did not know that even if one star in the zodiac breaks up and disappears we will not be able to know about it, for hundreds or millions of years, depending on its distance from the earth.

They also did not know that dead stars would be seen in the sky for several years till the last ray of radiant energy from it reaches us. It is such ignorant persons who propounded the pseudoscience of astrology. How many astrologers of today make sure that the stars and planets they see in the sky, when a child is born are really there in time and space?

On the basis of the velocity of light there is a difference of six minutes between the real and apparent positions of the planet Venus. This rule applies in varying degrees to the real and apparent positions of the sun, the moon, the planets and all the stars of the zodiacal constellations.

Thus the astrological charts prepared by these quacks can be out of date, anything from minutes, to millions of years.

Does the destiny of a person depend on the time of his birth? Child-birth is a mechanical occurrence that takes place 280 days after conception. It is possible for births to take place earlier or by surgical operation. If destinies of persons depend on the time of their births, it will be possible to plan human destinies by inducing their births to take place at auspicious or inauspicious times by medical manipulation. If so, gynocologist can hope to get better practice in future!

Astrologers of ancient Babylon and Greece used to prepare horoscopes based on the time of conception calculating back from the time of births. Hindu mythology records that the mystic Poonthanum was born as a result of a Brahmin astrologer cohabitting with a stranger woman because the Brahmin succeeded in convincing the woman that the planetary positions at the time were propitious and superbly suited to give birth to a child with divine qualities.

Unquestionably, astrology fails as a science. Its basic assumptions are illusory. A planet does not rise in the night sky, instead, the earth turns towards the planet. Planets are never really in conjunction. They remain millions of miles apart, no matter how close they appear in perspective. Aside from very slight changes in light, gravitation and magnetism from the sun and the moon, the planets do not affect the earth at all. The astrologer's so-called vibrations never make the needle of any instrument on earth quiver. In short, astrology produces results no more reliable than simple guess work.

That is why I have made my open challenge to astrologers all over the world, to remain open till my death. Astrologers themselves are aware that all their predictions are mere guess work. That is the reason why not a single astrologer is prepared to accept my challenge.

What then keeps astrology so much alive? For one thing, its apparatus of fascinating symbols, mysterious charts and abstruse calculations give it a scientific appearance, which dazzles many simple souls. Furthermore,astrologers are experts at telling people what they want to hear. Who does not like to hear that he is masterful and high-minded? Or that the next few months will bring him fame and fortune? Of whom is it not true that "Opportunity appeals to you most, when it gives you a chance to show your special ability?" Thus the astrologer hedges his analysis or predictions: whatever the facts, he can nearly always argue that he was right. His predictions are worded in ambiguous terms so that they could be interpreted suitably after the incident.

Every human being likes to be able to blame his failures on events beyond his control. It is consoling to be told that you have lost your job or your mate, not because of your stupidity or weakness of character, but because of cosmic events. It is ever more conforting to be told that your problems will soon be solved.

Although astrology furnishes no true guide to the characters or fortunes of men, and although its pretensions to science are false, it will continue to flourish as long as there are gullible fools in this world. Astrologers give their clients excuses for the past, praise for the present and hope for the future.

On scientific analysis it is found that about 6 per cent of the astrological predictions are significantly correct. This is what we should expect by the operation of the law of chance. A nonastrologer also will be able to obtain such a chance successfully.

I spent two years of my university days learning astrology from the Hora Sastra. When my son was born in 1927 I called him Aries because his lagna was the zodiacal Aries. I myself prepared the child's horoscope. According to that horoscope the child was not to have any brothers and sisters. I have no other children either legitimate or illegitimate. This striking prediction is enough to make any average person shout from the housetop about the genuiness of astrology:

Though I do not claim to be a scientist, my scientific mind did not allow me to give publicity to this one success in my astrological predictions, because all the other predictions in that horoscope have not come true. Human mind has an inherent weakness to forget all the failures and to remember the few lucky strikes. At the time when astrology originated, the earth was considered to be a flat disc, covered by a hemispherical dome—the sky—where the gods were supposed to have their homes. It was natural to think that the motion of the planets on the dome was regulated by gods. As the life of men were supposed to be ruled by the gods, it was believed that their destinies could be found by the study of the positions of the planets. We now know that the earth is a sphere, round which there are regular aeroplane and space satellite routes. Also we know now, that the motion of planets are not regulated by gods, but obey the natural laws discovered by Kepler and Newton. Moreover man has visited the moon several times in recent years, and unmanned spacecrafts studied Venus and Mars at close quarters. Samples of the moon are with us. Our scientific studies are revealing the absurdities of primitive beliefs of the astrologers.

I have with me a large collection of astrological predictions made by so-called eminent astrologers of various countries. My analysis of such predictions have clearly shown that none of those astrologers have scored anything above the operation of simple chance.

In February 1966, while walking with my wife along a main road at Trichi in South India, I was attracted by the sign board of an astrologer. As a person deeply interested in investigating all types of alleged para-normal phenomena, I walked into the presence of the astrologer. There I saw a bearded elderly person seated cross-legged on the floor with the upper part of the body smeared with holy ash. The trident marking on the forehead indicated that he was a Vaishnavite. He had a pile of old ola leaves in front, and a green parrot in a cage by the side. Scattered on the floor there were hundreds of cardboard squares with numbers written on them.

I entered into a long conversation with the astrologer and collected a lot of information about his trade. The astrologer said that those old olas—most of them crumbling at the edges—came down to him as heirloom from his ancestors. They were written by sages of old and contained the horoscopes of all humans born and yet to be born in this world. He said that my horoscope too with the full details of my past, present and future births could be found in one of the leaves in the pile. It could be reached either from the date of birth or by the help of the parrot.

I was told that my horoscope could be found by making a cash offering of any amount. Though the astrologer was not much pleased at the extremely small amount (one rupee) offered by me, he accepted it and let the parrot out among the card-board squares. The bird picked up in its beak the square with the number 37. He got the card-board in his hand, gave a grain of paddy to the bird both as a reward as well as to fix the conditioned reflex. After putting the parrot back into the cage he looked at the number on the card and pulled out the ola which contained my horoscope. I got the leaf in my hand and found that it was written in Tamil, a language I could not read. Though the astrologer got ready to read the horoscope and interpret it, I asked him to put it back in the pile.

I paid one more rupee and asked the astrologer to let the parrot out once more. The astrologer was reluctant to do it again, but under pressure and persuasion he let the parrot out. This time it picked up he card with the number 109. Thus ended the Trichi astrologer's Ola reading.

While astrologers are mostly deluded persons, I cannot say so about those who claim to possess Olas or Saptha Rishi Vakiam containing the horoscopes of all people dead, living and yet to be born, written by Rishis of old. They are utter frauds, because such a thing is a physical impossibility.

## Chapter 7

## *DECEPTIVE PERCEPTIONS*

Recently I happened to read in an Indian journal an article by Sri K. P. Kesava Menon written on his 83rd birthday. Sri Menon was a former High Commissioner of India in Ceylon, a writer, a patriot and one of India's foremost journalists. Even in his old age, whatever he writes is read avidly and taken as words of wisdom by millions in India. I quote below the translation of a small passage from that article: —

"A person's faith takes its shape from his own experience. Is it right to deny the experience of another person simply because you have failed to get the same experience? When I look at the sky at night, I am not able to see even a single star there, because I am now blind. If a person seated next to me revels at the splendour of the millions of stars he sees in the same sky, shall I be right in accusing him that he is telling a lie? If another person who is looking through a telescope, describes about still more stars he is able to see, will it be right on my part to say that they are purely the result of his imagination? Ordinary men do not have the physical strength of a Sandow or a Joe Louis. These strong men do not have the intelligence of a Ramanujan or Einstein. If it is so, is it not possible for some persons to have more spiritual powers and more spiritual experiences than others. It is my faith which gives me peace and happiness. Similarly if others also may derive peace and happiness through other types of faiths, why should I try to shake their beliefs?"

What Sri Menon says, though very misleading, may appear to be sound arguments even to many intelligent thinkers.

Let us have a psychological evaluation, and analysis of mental experiences and beliefs of man.

Experiences or perceptions are of two types—subjective and objective. Objective perceptions, like that of the person seeing the stars in the sky, either by the naked-eye-observation, or through a telescope, are true and factual, because they can be verified by others also. Subjective experiences, on the other hand, may be true, but need not necessarily be factual, and are not always amenable to reason and verification.

A young boy may be suffering from enurisis—that is the habit of urinating on the bed in sleep. He may be getting severe scolding every morning from his ignorant parents. What really happens in this boy's case is, drop by drop urine is filtered out of the kidneys, and get collected in his urinary bladder. When the bladder is full, this information is taken to the brain through the sensory nerves as electrical impulses These impulses conjure up a dream in the mind of the child. In his dream he gets up from his bed, goes to the urinal and urinates there. The whole thing is only a dream. The fact is that the boy has urinated on the bed itself.

If one early morning, before the child is awake, some one in the house lifts him up and removes the wet bed sheet or mat, and spreads a dry one, and the child is laid back still asleep, on awakening, as usual he will look with anxiety on the bed. On seeing that everything perfectly dry, he will jump up out of the bed with joy, and run up to the mother and say, "Mummy, last night I did not urinate on the bed. I went out and did it in the urinal".

This child is speaking the absolute truth, but it is not factual. It is absolutely true because it is a subjective experience of the child. But it is not factual, because on verification, the facts will show that the child did urinate on the bed. It is a deceptive experience, and it must not be given any credence.

Deceptive experiences or perceptions can be of three types: Illusion, Hallucination and Delusion.

Of these three deceptive perceptions, illusions are false sensory experiences. Hallucinations, on the other hand, are false mental experiences caused by physical, chemical, biological and psychological stimuli. Delusions, the third type, are false notions implanted in the mind by indoctrination and brainwashing.

Let us take the illusions first. They can be of five types, depending on the five senses. Optical or visual illusion, auditory illusions, tactile illusions, olfactory illusions and oral or lingual illusions.

Appearance of watery patches at a distance on a tarred road on a hot bright day is an optical illusion known as mirage. It may appear to be real from a distance. Only on verification by going near it we will know the illusory nature of a mirage.

The sweet taste of water when drunk just after eating the Indian Gooseberry, known locally as Nelli, is an oral illusion. The reality that this water is not sweet, but only an illusory experience, can be verified by making others who have not eaten Nelli, to drink it.

Many persons whose minds are deluded with the belief in non-existing ghosts, demons, satan, angels, gods, fairies, goblins, etc., may see them at night or in dark places as a result of optical illusions. Due to the fear artificially created by brainwashing from childhood, most persons will not have the courage to go near and verify the truth about these apparitions. All those who have conducted investigations courageously and scientifically have come to know that such apparitions are either due to optical illusions, or mental hallucinations.

The juggling feats of magicians, and the so-called miracles of imposters in the garb of holy men, are all optical illusions. Neither the magician nor the miracle-performing so-called holy men will allow any one to examine their bodies and dresses for fear of their conjuring tricks, or frauds being exposed.

Now let us turn our attention to hallucinations. As mentioned earlier, hallucinations are abnormal or deceptive mental experiences resulting from physical, chemical, biological and psychological causes.

Physical Stimuli: Doctors Walter Hess of Switzerland, J. Delgado of Yale University, and James Olds of Michigan University have succeeded in creating artificially emotions such as rage, fear, hunger, sorrow, sleep, melancholia, jubilation, love, eroticism, anxiety, aggression, extroversion, introversion, friendliness, hatred, pain, pleasure etc., by stimulating the various controls of the brain by electrical impulses, exactly like what happens in normal life.

Rhythmical sensory stimulations like drumming, clapping of hands in unison, chanting of refrains, singing.

poetry recitation, slogan-shouting, during mass demonstrations, dancing, physical jerks, alternate flashing of light and darkness into the eye, looking intensely on psychodellic patterns, bright flames, crystals and black spots on white b ack-ground the usual practice adopted by light reader, crystal gazers, and anjanakarayas—can cause hallucinatory experiences in the subject.

The bizzare behaviour of persons during devil dances, voodoo dances, Rock'n Roll, Baila, Twist, Kavadi dance, Kolam dance, temple poojas, revival meetings and pentecostal sessions, cricket matches, fire-walking, pop music etc., are all due to the rhythmical stimulations of the nervous system.

Then comes the Chemical Stimulations. Even from primitive times our forefathers knew the technique of producing hallucinations by consuming toddy, arrack, opium, ganja, and Dathura, which, in Sinhalese is known as Aththana and in Tamil as Poomathair.

The Balagi Temple in Muthumudali Street in Madras is famous among Hindus in Tamil Nadu, because of the unusual religious ecstasy experienced by devotees who take part in the pooja and the prasadam there.

Prasadam is a sacred ambrosia distributed by the priests among the devotees in return for their offerings. On 7th May, 1963, the chief priest of this temple was arrested for possessing 3960 grains of Ganja. During the trial it transpired that this priest was in the habit of adding Ganja to the prasadam. This priest, of course, knew the technique of producing religious experience with the help of Ganja.

In recent times, numerous hallucinatory drugs like Lysergic acid Dithalamide or L.S.D. to be sort, Marijuana, Heroine, Mescaline etc., are used as mental boosters, and Lagerctil, librium, vallium, Miltown, Amital Sodium etc., as mental sedatives or hypnogens. Dr. Albert Hoffman describes his own experience after taking a small dose of L.S.D. thus: "I saw my own spirit getting out of my body. It remained suspended in space, and I was looking on my own dead body and crying."

One-millionth grain of L.S.D. can induce in a person transcient hallucinations causing ecstasy and schizophrenia, which often gives rise to religious experiences. The discovery of chemical substances of the L.S.D. group in the blood-stream of schizophrenics and persons suffering from religio-mania made Doctor Quastel and Doctor Wheatly to conclude that the hallucinatory experiences of visionaries, ascetics, mystics, sadhus and the devotees who enter into trance at religious ceremonies and devil dances are all due to the derangement of their body chemistry.

Now, we will consider the third stimuli—the biological causes: Professors Orlando Miller and Allen Fisher, both of Canada, have discovered that certain abnormal behaviour patterns in men are associated with their chromosomal abnormalities. Men with pre-dominating sadistic tendencies have 22 pairs of XX chromosomes, and one XYY chromosome, instead of the normal 22 pairs of XX chromosome and one of XY chromosome.

Mental disturbances can also be caused by acute shortage of certain vitamins and enzymes in the body. The disease known as Beri Beri is caused by an acute shortage of Vitamin B. Insane behaviour is an important symptom of this disease. Mental derangement is also associated with another Vitamin-difficiency disease known as Pellagra. Such persons can be brought back to sanity by the administration of the Vitamin—Nocotinic acid.

Like vitamins and enzymes, imbalance of certain hor mones—the secretion of endocrinal glands—also can produce mental abnormalities. Persons who suffer from an insufficient supply of parathyroxine—the hormone secreted by the parathyroid gland—are subject to severe hallucinations.

A niece of mine who used to see my dead mother's spirit whenever she looked towards the sky, was brought by me to Ceylon from my ancestral home in Kerala. After a thorough medical check-up, it was discovered that she had a defective parathyroid. To rectify this deficiency she was given an extra dose of calcium. With the rectification of her body chemistry, ended the appearance of my mother's spirit before her.

Now let us consider the psychological causes. It is a well-known fact in psychology that human mind is susceptible to suggestions. These suggestions can be by auto-hypnosis, otherwise known as auto-suggestion, or by hetero-hypnosis. Just as many mental disorders can be cured by hypnotism, it is possible to induce psychic and psycho-somatic ailments by hypnotic suggestions.

Religious indoctrination and brainwashing are slow and continuous process of hypnosis. Talking like a possessed person, often in a changed voice and fabricated language —this in psychology is known as glossolalia—ecstatic trance during poojas and devil dances, healing by faith, prayer, poojas, pilgrimages, blessings, annointing, sacrifice, charm, offerings, drinking or bathing in so-called holy waters etc., are nothing but the effects of auto—or hetero-hypnosis on the subject's suggestible mind.

Deep meditation and chanting of refrains have self-hypnotising effects. Utterances of persons in deep meditation or trance, are nothing but the hallucinations of deranged minds, and should not be regarded as divine revelations or occult messages. L.S.D. and Ganja also can produce the same effect. Neurotics and psychotics in meditation, who claim to have received divine revelations, who claim to have achieved enlightenment, who claim to possess paranormal miraculous powers, and those who profess to possess the power to know all the secrets of the unknown and the unknowable, are all fit subjects for the psychiatrist's couch, and not saints and sages to be adored, worshipped or counselled. Diversity in religions is due to the diversity of the hallucinations of their respective founders.

Lastly let us consider the third type of deceptive perceptions: the Delusions:—

Delusions are accumulated false beliefs resulting from indoctrination and brainwashing from impressionable age Belief in ghosts, demons, satan, angels, gods, astrology; palmistry, numerology, necromancy, charms, curses, blessings, Seth Kavi, Vas Kavi, omens, sacrifices, pirith nool, pilgrimages, anjana eliya, light reading, card reading, tumbler talk, clairvoyance, clairaudience, telepathy, precognition, telekinesis, manthras, holy persons, holy placcs, holy objects, holy times, holy waters, hell, heaven, rebirth, purgatory, materialisation, levitation, transmigration etc., are some of our delusions.

As Shri Menon says, it may be that some persons may derive mental peace and happiness by his or her blind beliefs. Similar results, no doubt, can be obtained by consuming L.S.D., Ganja, opium, toddy or kasippu also! But it is not a question whether any type of experience Induces peace or happiness, but whether it is true.

## Chapter 8

### *ENLIGHTENMENT THROUGH MEDITATION!*

I feel strongly that some of the misleading statements of Prof. I. G. Hewage in his article on "Panadure Controversy and the Buddhist Society" (CDN, 12-8-1973) should not be left unchallenged. His description in glorious terms of the highly dangerous fad known as yogic, contemplative or transcendental meditation as a means to 'achieve knowledge, enlightenment, intellectual development, self-realisation, perfect mental health, parapsychic powers, physical luminescence etc.,' is liable to misguide the masses, especially as it comes from the pen of a university don.

Except some behavioural patterns known as instincts, man has to acquire all his knowledge through the objective experiences of his five senses subsequent to his birth, and not through meditation. A person devoid of the five senses from birth will live only like a vegetable without any knowledge whatsoever. If knowledge can be achieved through meditation, as Prof. Hewage says, we should scrap all educational institutions in the country, and establish meditation centres in their places! Why spend a large amount for education?

Unlike the objective perceptions through the senses, the subjective perceptions of a person can be unreal and deceptive. For example, the hallucinations of a psychotic are only his subjective experiences without any reality behind them.

Hallucinations can be induced in a person by chemical, physical, biological and psychological causes. Narcotic drugs and intoxicants; sensory stimulants like rhythmical drumming, clapping of hands, chanting or refrains and mantras, singing and dancing; imbalance of hormones, vitamins and enzymes in the body; fear, shock, hetero-hypnosis, auto-hypnosis etc., can induce hallucinations in feeble-minded persons.

A Tamil gentleman working in the printing department at Lake House was once brought to me in an insane condition by his Sinhalese wife for hypnotic treatment. Investigations revealed that yogic meditation was the cause of his insanity.

This man happened to read a book in Tamil on 'Yogic Meditation'. He read in it that a person could get his 'mental eye' opened to have clairvoyant and precognitive visions if he is to sit in Padmasana and recite the mantra "Om Reem Jayamana Sakti" 108 times.

He decided to give it a trial. One night he sat cross-legged on his bed and started chanting Om Reem Jayamana Sakti, Om Reem Jayamana Sakti. . . . According to his wife's version, he could not finish the full course of the chant. After chanting the refrain fifty or sixty times he started running about the house shouting "Muruga, Muruga. . .' From that night he was behaving like a mad man, undergoing treatment from several kattadiyas.

Books on psychiatry are replete with similar cases. Bizarre behaviour of devotees at temple poojas, devil dances, revival meetings, pop sessions, mass demonstrations etc., are due to temporary insanity induced by drumming, chanting of Bhajans and refrains, dancing, singing, slogan shouting etc.

The religious fad known as meditation is a slow process inducing auto-hypnosis. Hallucinatory experiences of persons in meditation are often according to their religious delusions. A Christian in meditation might have the hallucination of seeing Jehovah seated on a golden throne in heaven with Jesus on his right, and surrounded by numerous winged angels singing halleluyah. A Hindu or Buddhist, on the other hand, may have the hallucinations of his previous and future births. LSD, Mescalin, Ganja, Peyoti etc., also can induce similar hallucinations.

Some persons in transcendental meditation can become victims of cryptesthesia—a neurotic condition in which the patient gets obsessed with the foolish idea that he had occult, psychic and supernatural powers.

When illiterate and ignorant persons suffer from mental aberrations, they are branded as lunatics, and nobody attaches any value to what they say. On the other hand if the victim of hallucinations happens to be a talented intellectual, he may be able to convince his hearers and readers that he has experienced superconsciousness, ultimate reality, enlightenment, oneness with god, self-realisation etc., and it may be that he will have numerous devotees and disciples. Mentally deranged persons of extraordinary ability and intelligence often become founders and preachers of religions.

Like narcotic drugs, meditation should be banned and made illegal because both have the same effect on human mind.

Prof. Hewage says that an aura of light emanates from the body of a person in meditation, and this 'can be perceived by the meditator himself although 'you and I don't see it'. He then continues: "As they don't see them, some learned rationalists who don't believe in anything they don't see here and now, tend to say that they are not rational".

What an absurd statement is this? Although they can't see infra-red and ultra-violet rays, atoms and molecules, oxygen and hydrogen with their eyes, rationalists do not reject their existence because they know that it is possible to establish the existence of these invisible things by scientific verification.

How ludicrous it is to say that an aura of light emanates 'from a person who has attained the fifth stage on the path of purity' at the testimony of a meditating psychopath, although sober persons do not see it! It is as ridiculous as accepting what a schizophrenic at a mental hospital says as true just because he is a man of high academic qualifications, and rejecting what his nursing attendant says because he has no such qualification.

As additional proof of the emanation of light from the body of the meditator Prof. Hewage directs his readers to the text and pictures in the book "Psychic Discoveries behind the Iron Curtain" written by two American women. It is strange that the professor failed to see similar corona of light round the pictures of leaves and buds in the same book. Do plants also meditate and 'attain the fifth stage on the path of purity' to- emanate aura of light?

Scientists do not see anything mysterious in the corona round infra-red photographs of live tissues of animals or plants. Such coronas are due to temperature variation, and not due to light emanation!

Confirming telepathy, Prof. Hewage says that words "were transmitted telepathically from mind-to-mind across four hundred miles of space". He visualises the "possibilities of communication of important messages in space flight and for the benefit of submarines" He also says that telepathic faculty can be developed through meditation.

Telepathy being a phenomenon that can be verified by any one, why depend on dubious anecdotes from books and newspapers? All my attempts in the past in testing claimants of telepathy and clairvoyance have produced only negative results. Can Prof. Hewage produce a single person from any part of the world—even from behind the Iron curtain—who can read the mind of a person, not in space or submarines, but just close by in an adjacent room?

The story of the successful experiment in transmitting messages through telepathy from Duke University, North Carolina, under the guidance of Prof. J. B. Rhine of parapsychology fame, to the atomic submarine Nautilus 1200 miles away and hundreds of feet under the ocean was first published in 1959. It continued to be copied and published in several newspapers all over the world till 1963 when, the American magazine "THIS WEEK" did a little private investigation.

What the then captain of Nautilus, Captain William R. Anderson told the editor of "This Week" was thus:

"Although the Nautilus was engaged in a verv wide variety of activities. certainly these did not include experiments in telepathy. The report about the telepathy experiment by Messers Pouwels and Bergier is completely false. During that time Nautilus was in fact high and drv in dock at Portsmouth, undergoing her first overhaul".

Colonel William Bowers of the U.S. Air Force, whose participation in this submarine telepathy was reported, declared:

"The experiment in which I was alleged to have participated never took place. I have never been assigned to the Westinghouse Laboratory where the check up of the results of the telepathic experiment was reported to have been carried out. In fact, on July 25th, 1959, I was assigned to duties in the Air University, Alabama, which was in no way related to extra-sensory investigations."

In short, as "This Week" commendably makes clear, this submarine ESP story was a big hoax. But that will not prevent it from staying around for quite a time, to be cited as proof by ESP faddists like Prof. Hewage.

Unlike fiction writers, university dons should try to be factual about what they write.

## Chapter 9

# *THE MIRACLE OF GANG A WATER*

Kerala, the land of my birth, is very similar to Sri Lanka in its topography, climate, fauna, flora and even the cultural and ethnic qualities of its people. As in Sri Lanka, witchcraft and devil dances thrive even to this day among the villagers in Kerala. More than half a century ago, when I was a young boy, it was a common practice to resort to witchcraft whenever anything untoward happened in the family. Most householders, as a result of superstitious beliefs, treasured some sort of 'sacred' medicine or talisman which, they imagined, could effect magical cures for all their ailments. For the Nairs it was the 'sacred' water—theertham—from the holy river Ganges, brought by pilgrims who returned from the 'sacred' city of Benares. For Syrian Christians it was often the sanctified oil from Antioch or the 'sacred' water from Lourdes. For the Muslims it was the water sanctified by the container made to touch the 'sacred' Kaaba stone at Mecca brought yearly by the Haj pilgrims.

From 1921 to 1924 my younger brother the late Dr. Behanan T. Kovoor of the Yale University, US., and I were students at the University of Calcutta. The city of Calcutta is about 1500 miles from my native town Tiruvalla. It took about five days for us to reach Calcutta by train.

A trip from Tiruvalla to the distant city on the banks of the river Ganges, by two young boys in search of higher education was an unusual event those days among the people of our neighbourhood. Because of the long distance and the heavy expense involved, we used to come home only once a year during the long mid-summer vacation.

## CEREMONIAL SEND-OFF

Our departure to Calcutta after the holidays was a ceremonial affair. Days before our departure, both my brother and I were feted by our neighbours. During the last few days of our holidays we had practically all our meals in the neighbouring houses irrespective of caste, creed or class. Almost all the Nair families wanted us to bring for them, when we returned, at least a few drops of 'theertham' (Ganges water). For them, we were extremely fortunate because even in our boyhood we would be getting a chance of bathing in the 'sacred' waters of the 'holy' Ganges, and thus attain 'moksha' without much effort.

On the day of departure, our house and courtyard used to get crowded with men, women and children from the neighbouring houses. The men folk in our neighbourhood, who were mostly farmers and petty landlords, kept away from their normal work that day for the sake of bidding us farewell.

After prayers and blessings by our family priest the Rev. K. P. Thomas, a beloved cousin of mine, our mother insisted that we went round to all the elderly men and women in the group to receive their blessings, which they did by placing their hands on our foreheads, with tears rolling down their cheeks. Many women used to burst out into loud weeping. The sympathetic effect of their weeping on our tender minds made us also shed tears. It was really a touching separation, the effect of which used to linger in our minds throughout the whole journey. Fortunately, on reaching Calcutta, the multifarious attractions of the big city and the boisterous life in our hostel made us forget fast all about the home and our good neighbours. Such thoughts came back to our minds only when the time for our return trip approached during the next summer.

## THE GANGES

The river Ganges which has its source in the 'sacred' Kailas (Himalayas) flows down the Gangetic plain for about 1500 miles and falls into the Bay of Bengal. It is in flood throughout the summer months when the snow on the Himalayas melt. Since it is a fast-flowing river, its water is always muddy.

During my long stay in Bengal I bathed in this river only once. It became my first and last bath in that river because of a shocking experience I had on that occasion. As I lifted my head out of the water after a long immersion my head came in contact with a white and slimy object. It turned out to be a highly decomposed dismembered human hand, partially eaten away by fish. It made me sick, and I had to go without food for a couple of days.

Though prohibited by law at present, during the days of my youth it was the usual practice among the Hindus of North India to ceremoniously deposit the dead bodies of their dear ones into the 'sacred' waters of this holy river. By this they insured 'moksha' for their departed souls. Those who lived far away from this river had to be satisfied by throwing the ashes into it after cremation. More than half a century ago one could see at any time numerous floating carcases flowing down this river in various stages of decomposition. Thousands of dead bodies were dumped into this so-called sacred river every day at hundreds of cities, towns and villages along the banks of this long river. Yet, millions of pilgrims from all over India 'purify' themselves by not only bathing in it, but also by drinking the polluted water. I have seen devotees pushing away carcases which come their way, and continue their ablutions. They were brainwashed from childhood into the belief that in spite of the presence of decomposing carcases in it, the water of the Ganges is pure and 'sacred'.

As a result of the abhorrence after my first nauseous experience in this 'holy' river, I decided not to take even a drop of water from it to my good neighbours. Since Behanan and I were reluctant to disappoint them, we decided to substitute some good well water for the Ganges water.

The nearest Railway Station to Tiruvalla those days was Kottarakkara. When we got down from the train at Kottarakkara we used to fill two bottles with drinking water from the filter in the waiting room, cork them properly and keep them along with our luggage. From that time onwards the water in the two bottles was called 'theertham'.

To reach Tiruvalla we had to travel about 36 miles by transport bus. There were many buses running on this route, all belonging to different operators. There was much rivalry and competition among those bus operators. This competition was a boon for the passengers as they received very polite and liberal treatment from them. As there was no governmental control over bus transport those days, buses came and went at unscheduled times, took whichever routes the driver liked, stopped whenever the passengers wanted, and cancelled trips according to the whims and fancies of the operators. To make sure of their fare the conductors and cleaners of the few buses at the Kottarakkara Railway Station used to struggle among themselves to put the luggages of the waiting passengers on the hood of their own buses. Once the luggage was on the top of their bus, they were sure that the owner of the luggage would get into their bus.

When the conductors and cleaners handledour luggage roughly in their struggle to secure their fare, we used to beg them to be extra careful about the handling of the two bottles of 'theertham'. The word 'theertham' had an electrifying effect on them as well as the other fellow passengers. They handled the two bottles with due respect, and saw that both of us were given specially reserved seats by the side of the driver. Finally, on reaching Tiruvalla, the bus is diverted from the normal route with the sardine-packed passengers in it, and driven to an extra distance of about two miles to drop us at Kovoor house. After dropping our luggage and us at home the conductor produced a small phial with the humble request for a small quantity of the theertham to be shared among the driver, the cleaner and himself.

## MIRACLE CURES

We used to entrust the two bottles of theertham to our devoted Christian mother. With pride and pleasure she used to distribute the theertham to our Nair neighbours according to their needs. Till the death of our beloved mother in 1942 she was not told the real truth about the theertham. During the first two days of our arrival home, our neighbours used to flow in to greet us and to get their share of' the sacred water.

Next mid-summer too the same fraud was repeated with all solemnity. Thus, for four consecutive years we continued to cheat our Christian mother and the Hindu neighbours with the 'Kottarakkara Railway Station Water', and every holiday we had to give patient hearing to the numerous accounts of miraculous cures effected by the previous year's supply.

Puthur Raman Nair had this to say: "During the last two years we had no need to seek medical help. My mother had a severe attack of diarrhoea last April. I just gave her a spoonful of honey with two drops of theertham in it. That was all. Within three hours she was perfectly cured."

Kilannaparampil Lakshmi Amma said, "Every time my daughter got cold or fever, a single drop of the theertham gave her perfect relief. I was subject to severe migraine since I had a miscarriage three years ago. Now when I get any symptom of the headache coming on, I simply apply a drop of the theertham on my forehead, and it stops with that. Even if it comes, the pain is onlv very slight."

Vettvelil Parukutty who had two difficult and complicated child-births when she gave birth to her first two children, had a very easy one at home when her third child was born. All what she did at the third time was to take two drops of the theertham immediately when the labour pain started.

Oliprakkatu Narayana Kuruppu proved the miraculous power of the theertham by an experimental research. He had two grafted mango trees in his garden. Both were of the same stock and of the same age. During the dry season he watered the two trees. Once he added a few drops of the theertham to the water he poured for one of the trees. When the flowering season arrived, the tree which got a dose of the theertham flowered, while the other tree produced only a crop of tender leaves.

Chankroth Patchu Pillai immunised all the members of his family by pouring spoonful of the theertham in to the family well. Since taking this precaution not a sing le member of the Chankroth family fell ill.

There were numerous similar stories of miracles narrated by our neighbours who came to repeat their request for a further supply.

## EXPLANATION

The belief in miraculous powers of holy water is very ancient. Men in every walk and clime have maintained superstitious beliefs in the miraculous powers of sacred and holy objects, persons, places and times. Apart from the psychological effects of suggestion on their minds, there is absolutely no evidence to show that there are objective merits in such beliefs. Just as beneficial effects can be had by hypnotic suggestions, it is possible to have harmful effects also by such suggestions or beliefs. Many of the neurotic subjects at mental hospitals are the final results of diverse types of superstitious beliefs. He who believes in sacredness is sure to get mentally tormented by acts of desecration too. Psychology tells us that such mental traumas are the causes of neurotic afflictions, mostly among the credulous and mentally feeble types. Among the numerous neurotics brought to me, I have found by statistics that the prevalence of neurosis among communities is directly proportional to the extent of superstitious beliefs held by them. Even in such communities, there are more women neurotics than men for same reason. Better education for girls, and relaxation of the strict observance of the purdah, can help to a great extent to reduce neurosis among women.

A present Deputy Director of Education, was some years ago teaching at Jaffna Central College, where I too was a teacher. One day he drank some water from a 'kooja' kept in the staff room. A few hours later another teacher drained the last quantities of water from that kooja into a glass tumbler. Out came a small dead snake along with the water. The Director who heard about it became violently sick. The nausea was continuous, and we got alarmed. Finally, it stopped abruptly when he was convinced that the water he drank was from another kooia which was on the same table. Though the water he drank was from the same kooia, his nausea stopped when he was made to believe blindly that he drank from another. This shows how one can get sick and get cured psychologically. But to argue that sickness which is not psycho-somatic in origin can be cured by faith is absurd.

The 'Kottarakkara Railway Station Water' did not do any miracle in our neighbourhood. Our neighbours' anecdotes simply showed the credulous nature of those simple folks who were brainwashed from childhood about the miraculous properties of the theertham. Discarding logic and reason, their conditioned minds only attempted to give interpretations and explanations to suit their blind beliefs.

The so-called beneficial effects of sacrifices, pilgrimages, offerings, prayers, blessings, worships, vows, consecrations, dedications, ordinations, 'Lourdes water', theerthams, prasadams, sacraments, baptism, anointing of holy ash. yagna, pooja etc., are merely subjective experiences without any objective reality. Similarly curse, charms, 'vas kavi' hoonyams, ill omens, inauspicious times, horoscopes, evil spells etc., can be harmful only to gullible fools.

Academic education and intelligence need not be considered as marks of non-gullibility. In fact, some of the highly educated persons in exalted positions are extremely gullible, even resorting to witchcraft. It is only persons capable of rational thinking who can free themselves from credulity. Blind believers are mentally blind in spite of their intelligence and education.

## Chapter 10

## *THE MIND READING HORSE*

Mr. J. B. Rhine is a biologist who has become world-famous by his dubious researches in equally dubious subjects like telepathy (thought-reading), clairvoyance (extra-sensory perception), pre-cognition (fore-knowledge of events) and psychokinesis (motion effected by thought). He worked in collaboration with his wife Dr. Louisa E. Rhine and Dr. Helge Lundholm under the world-renowned psychologist Professor William McDougall at Duke University, North Carolina.

Dr. J. B. Rhine's writings in his books "New Frontiers of Mind", "The Reach of Mind", "Extra-sensory perception" and the "Journal of Para-Psychology" confirming the occurrence of psychic powers such as telepathy, clairvoyance, pre-cognition and psychokinesis in some 'gifted' persons are authoritatively quoted by believers in psychic phenomena.

Eminent research scientists like Dr. Eugene Adams, Dr. George R. Price, Professor Kennedy, Professor John Scarne, Dr. John E. Coover and others have severely criticised, condemned and even challenged Rhine's experiments and findings.

Dr. Adams of Colgate University reports, "I have completed a series of 30,000 individual tests of the card guessing sort that Dr. Rhine has conducted at Duke University. My tests were designed to test clairvoyance, telepathy and the two in combination. I used the same cards that Rhine did, and I repeated his general technique. My results were negative."

Dr. G. R. Price of Minnesota University in an article in the 'Science' of August 25th, 1955 attacked severely the so-called psychic experiments of Dr. Rhine.

Dr. John E. Coover, Professor of Psychology at Stanford University, California, announced that after 10,000 tests he had obtained no better than chance results, and thereby ruled out the existence of telepathy.

Writing about Extra-Sensory Perception, Professor John Scarne says, ". . . .all the evidence submitted by **Rhine** designed to prove the existence of psychic phenomena is a lot of humbug. ... It is an established fact that at one time or another every prominent psychic researcher has been duped by falling for some amateurish trick performed by a trickster operating under the guise of being psychic. Rhine's extra-sensory perception and psychokinesis are nothing but errors Let us stop kidding ourselves. If Rhine had one subject who possessed extra-sensory perception, he and that subject could win an enormous fortune inashort time".

## EXPERIMENTS

Professor Kennedy of Stanford University reports of his experiments and tests that failed to substantiate the findings of Dr. Rhine in regard to the existence of clairvoyance and telepathy. He declared, "One" of the scientific demands on truth is that when experiments are repeated in laboratories, results similar to the original shall be obtained. One hundred students were used in our tests, and our results did not correspond with those of Dr. Rhine".

It is indeed strange that Professor William McDougall with fifty years of experience in psychic research behind him, could not offer Rhine and Lundholm a wee bit of data on either modern or old experiments relating to psychic phenomena, instead of having them resort to tales and accounts of feats they heard and read were performed by the early mesmerists which dated back hundreds of years.

In Richmond, Virginia, one Mrs. C. D. Fonda owned a horse named 'Lady Wonder' reputed to possess psychic powers. In the Journal of 'Abnormal and Social Psychology', Volume 23 (1929), on page 449-466 there appeared an article headed "An investigation of a Mind Reading Horse" by J. B. Rhine and Dr. Louisa E. Rhine of Duke University. This article stated in parts:—

"The animal, subject of the experiment herein described, is a three-year old filly, Lady Wonder, owned by Mrs. C. D. Fonda of Richmond, Virginia. According to reports which led to our enquiry, the horse could make predictions, solve simple arithmetic problems, answer questions aptly and intelligently, and do all these without verbal commands. All what was needed was that the question be written down and shown to Mrs. Fonda. In Mrs. Fonda's opinion these accomplishments of the horse were due to a combination of unusual intelligence and the capacity for mind-reading."

"Our experiments were begun on December 3rd, 1927, and ended on January 15th, 1928, covering in this period a total of six days. The tests were made at the residence of Mrs. Fonda in a demonstration tent 9 x 12 feet.

"Professor William McDougall was present and participated in the experiments on two days, and the Assistant Superintendent of District Schools Mrs. John F. Thomas on one day. Others present were Mrs. C. D. Fonda, Dr. B. Rhine, Dr. Louisa E. Rhine".

So, Dr. Rhine after employing his great telepathy testing technique on Lady Wonder for six days aided by a number of his colleagues including his superior at Duke University Prof. William McDougall, and after taking one year's time to think over the matter and discuss with his colleagues, wrote:—

"There is left only the telepathic explanation, the transference of mental influence by an unknown process. Nothing was discovered that failed to accord with it, and no other hypothesis seems tenable in view of the results."

In plane language the above simply means that the scientists of the department of psychology of Duke University have stated in print their conclusion that Mrs. Fonda's horse was capable of reading a person's mind.

Lady Wonder, thanks to Dr. Rhine, became the most famous non-racing horse in the world, and helped her owner earnafabulous fortune. This wonderful story of Lady Wonder was featured in newspapers and magazines, including a spread in the LIFE magazine. The 1956 July issue of CHALLENGE credits Lady Wonder with aiding the police in finding the dead body of a young boy.

It is estimated that Lady Wonder, since the day that Dr. Rhine pronounced her psychic, has been seen and talked to by 150,000 visitors who came to seek her help to solve their problems.

As the fame of Lady Wonder reached Professor John Scarne in New Jersey, he decided to investigate the case himself. One afternoon Scarne visited Mrs. Fonda's farm in the company of Donald Grey. They waited till the crowd of people who were having their minds read, thinned out, and entered a tent in which there were Mrs. Fonda and the three year old filly Lady Wonder.

Lady Wonder was standing in front of a table on which were arranged several rows of lettered wooden blocks each showing one letter of the alphabet. Mrs. Fonda explained to Scarne and others there that Lady Wonder, after reading their minds, would answer the questions by spelling out the answers. She went on to explain that the horse's nose would touch one letter at a time and thereby spell out the answer to the question.

Scarne did not say a word but just tried to look interested in a police officer in uniform talking to the horse, This officer had come from Chicago to consult Lady Wonder to solve a bank robbery. He asked the horse, "Lady, do you know why I came".

Lady Wonder nosed the blocks and spelled out YES. He then asked in a nervous voice, "Lady Wonder, how shall I go about it?" Lady Wonder then nosed the letters WORK. The police officer then asked in a begging tone, "I am sorry Lady for asking so many questions, but please tell me where the robbers are at present". The horse then touched the letters CHI for Chicago. It could not complete the word because letter C would have to be used twice, which meant Mrs. Fonda would have to move the block C in its original position. She made it a practice never to come in front of the horse during performance.

The police officer then turned to the horse and said, "Thank you Lady. You have been of great help to me."

Mrs. Fonda then told Scarne to ask any question he wished. "How do I do that?" Scarne asked. Mrs. Fonda replied, just say, "Lady please tell me how did I come here?" Scarne repeated the question. Lady Wonder moved her head a bit, then dropped her head close to the lettered blocks on the table. After a few seconds of hesitation Lady's nose pushed the block marked C. She brought her head upward again, then down again and the nose pushed the block marked A. Next she pushed R. The three letters spelled out the word CAR.

After this demonstration of mind-reading by Lady Wonder Scarne turned to Mrs. Fonda and said, "That's wonderful, but I have a question I am thinking of that, I would like the Lady to answer. How do I ask her without telling her what the question is?"

Mrs. Fonda seemed stumped for a moment, then handed over a pad and pencil to Scarne and said, "Write your question on this pad, and don't let the Lady see it." Scarne wrote the question on the pad, but did so without Mrs. Fonda seeing it.

Mrs. Fonda looked a bit disappointed, but turned to Lady and asked her to answer Professor Scarne's question. The horse did not move its bead, and the reason was obvious to Scarne. After a few minute's wait Scarne realized that if Mrs. Fonda did not see his question, the horse was not going to push the blocks with her nose. So Scarne decided to let Mrs. Fonda get a glimpse of the question without his apparently knowing what she did. As Scarne turned to talk to his friend Grey, he surreptitiously turned over the pad so that Mrs. Fonda could read the question, which read "Where do I live?". Scarne turned around after he was convinced that Mrs. Fonda had seen the question, and immediately Lady Wonder started to push around the blocks and spelled the word NEW YORK.

Scarne acted surprised and said, "That is wonderful. How did Lady know that I lived in New York?" (Scarne actually lived in New Jersey). Scarne gave Mrs. Fonda her fee-five dollars-and left with Grey.

As Scarne was driving back he could not help but wonder if it were true that the Professor from the Duke University had been fooled by such an obvious bit of horseplay on the part of Mrs. Fonda. According to Scarne, the only clever thing with Mrs. Fonda and her mind-reading horse was Mrs. Fonda's salesmanship in duping the professor.

The simple fact of making Lady Wonder push the blocks with her nose at the proper time is explained by Scarne thus:—

"Mrs. Fonda carried a small whip in her right hand, and she cued the horse by waving it. I detected Mrs.

Fonda doing it every time the horse moved the lettered blocks with the nose. This method of doing the trick might have puzzled me if I hadn't known that the placement of Horse's eyes on either side of the head gave them wide backward range of peripheral vision. Therefore it offered no problem for me to detect.

"Mrs. Fonda, when cueing Lady Wonder, stood about two and a half feet behind, and approximately at a 60-degree angle to Lady's head. The shaking of the whip first time was signal for Lady to bend her head within a couple of inches to the blocks. A second shake of the whip was the cue for Lady to continuously move her head in a bent position back and forth over the blocks. When Lady Wonder's head was just above the desired block, Mrs. Fonda made the horse touch the block with her nose by shaking the whip a third time. It was simple as that."

(The Amazing World, pp. 247-53)

It does not surprise me that Professor William McDougall was duped by a tricker woman and her trained horse, but I am surprised that Dr. J. B. Rhine who is a biologist should have forgotten the fact that a horse with its laterally placed eyes could see what was taking place behind it.

With the publication of Professor Scarne's investigations came the end of Lady Wonder's mind reading career.

## Chapter 11

# *BIBLE IS A DANGEROUS MORAL GUIDE*

The All-Ceylon Buddhist Congress is insistent that religious instruction in schools is extremely necessary to guide the youths of this country in moral and cthical ways. The leaders of the diverse Christian sects also are equally insistent about teaching Bible to the Christian students.

I am writing this to show how dangerous a book the so-called Holy Bible is as a guide to moral and cthical training. Millions of Christians all over the world believe, without any valid evidence, that the Bible is the 'Word of God'. When there is no evidence that God exists, how can it be accepted that the Bible is the word of God? Even if it is proved that there is a God, that fact, would not in any way support the claim that he inspired the Bible.

Bible is not the only book that is claimed to be inspired by a god. Muslims claim that their sacred book—the Koran—also was inspired by their god, Allah.

The Moral precepts of Bible, the justice of its laws, its historical inaccuracies, the inexactitude of its science, and the absurdity of its philosophy makes this bock not acceptable to the 20th century man. Why talk about the inspiration of the Bible when we know what it teaches is not true? The truth is that the doctrine of inspiration is a myth invented by the Jewish and Christian priests. That the Bible is a human creation, altogether without divine authority is proved by the fact that'in the field of morals it is a very dangerous guide.

Let us have a look at some of its moral teachings.

### HONESTY

Truth-telling is one of the most precious of virtues, we cherish. But the Bible upholds deception and lying. In Jeremiah, chapter 20, verse 7, the writer complains,

'O God thou hast deceived me". In chapter 4, verse 10, Jeremiah has charged God with deception. He says, "Ah, Lord God, surely thou hast deceived the people of Jerusalem".

A striking instance of the divine falsehood is found in the 22nd chapter of 1st King, There it is said, "And the Lord said we shall persuade Ahab through a lying spirit. Behold the Lord hath put a lying spirit in the mouth of the prophets". No sensible person will advocate the teaching of these godly deception to the children during their impressionable age In an article like this it is not possible to cite the numerous falsehoods and inaccuracies of the Bible. The story of the deluge as given in the book of Genesis is full of falsehood and absurdities. In chapter 7 of Genesis it is said, "it rained for 40 days and 40 nights. It rained 15. cubits high and the mountains were covered".

A cubit being 1 foot and 6 inches, it means that the flood was 22½ ft. deep. Mount Everest is 29,002 ft. high, and Mount Ararat 17,260 ft. What a big falsehood it is for the god-inspired Bible to tell us that 22½ ft. of water covered these mountains! Can any sensible person believe the biblical lie that the giant animals of the earth like dinosaurs, mammoth and elephants got into the ark through the single door-cum-window 18 inches square?

Now let us look at the New Testament, a book claimed to be spotless for veracity. In the third chapter of Romans, St. Paul offered this astounding justification for falsehood. He says, "For if the truth of God hath more abounded through my lie unto his glory".

In second Corinthians Paul further acknowledges his use of falsehood in his teaching. He says, "Being crafty, I caught you with guile". According to Paul there is nothing wrong with lying when it is done in the service of God. But moral conduct demands truthfulness. A book that upholds lying and falsehood definitely is a dangerous moral guide.

How dishonest it was on the part of God to have asked Moses to tell a deliberate lie to Pharoah. In chapter 5 of Exodus we read, "Moses and Aaron came and said unto Pharoah thus said the Lord God of Israel, let my people go, that they may hold a feast unto me in the wilderness. Three days journey into the wilderness to make sacrifice unto me". Here we see a helpless god trying to get his own people out of slavery by telling a deliberate lie to Pharoah. Were the Israelites really going out just for three days, or for good never to return?

The world needs honesty no less than truth. The so-called Holy Bible teaches one to become a cheat, a thief and a despoiler of fellow beings! In the 3rd chapter of Exodus we have God's specific instruction to rob one's neighbour. He says, "I will give this people of Israel favour in the sight of the Egyptians, and it will come to pass that when you go, ye will not go empty handed. Every woman amongst you shall borrow of her neighbour's jewels of silver and jewels of gold, and raiments; and ye shall put them upon your sons and daughters, and ye shall spoil the Egyptians". The 12th chapter says, "And the children of Israel did according to the word of god, and they borrowed of the Egyptians jewels of silver and jewels of gold, and raiments; and the Lord gave the people favour in the sight of the Egyptians, so that they lent unto them such things as they required. And they ruined the Egyptians."

Are we to teach our boys and girls how to rob under the pretext of borrowing? Even if it is moral in the opinion of god of the Bible, we in Sri Lanka should not allow our children to be taught such immoral ideas. How can we expect honesty and truth among christians who are taught such immoralities through their scriptures?

It appears the god of Bible has no hesitation to make false promises. In Genesis 46, Verse 3 God is said to have spoken to Israel. (Jacob), "I am the God of thy father, fear not to go down into Egypt, for I will there make thee a great nation". In reality what happened? Instead of becoming a great nation, his descendents became slaves in Egypt. Is this Jehovah an omniscient?

## SLAVERY

One of the worst degrading chapters in human history is slavery and slave trade. Slavery denied to millions of men and women the right to live as human beings. It filled human lives with atrocities of the worst kind. Before the Bible was written tne inhabitted parts of the earth was blighted with slavery. The Bible came and what did it have to say about this appalling curse which reduced human beings to the level of beasts? We are told that the Bible is the message of God, of wisdom and love. Does it sound a clarion call to human freedom? On the other hand it only approves slavery. In the 21st chapter of Exodus, God gives the advice to the slave holder, "If thou buy an Hebrew servant, six years he shall serve, and in the seventh, he shall go out free for nothing. If he were married, then his wife shall go with him. If his master has given him a wife, and she has borne him sons and daughters, the wife and her children shall be his master's property, and he shall go out by himself. And if the servant shall plainly say, I love my wife and my children; I will not go out free, then his master shall bring him unto the judges, and his master shall bore his ear through with an awl, and he shall serve him for ever". Thus, according to biblical justice if a slave wantsto be with his own wife and children, he must be a slave throughout his life. God allows the slave holder to kill his slave and go unpunished. In the same chapter it is said, "If a master smites his servant of his maid with a rod, and he died under his hand, he shall be punished. Notwithstanding, if he continues to live a day or two, the master shall not be punished, for he is his money". Can a civilized man accept the teaching that one man is another man's money? The New Testament supports the Old Testament in binding the shackles to the limbs of the slave. In Ephesians 6, Verse 5, St: Paul says, "servants, be obedient to them that are your masters". The slave is commanded to cringe and crawl trembling at his master's feet.

## BIGOTRY AND INTOLERANCE

We in the 20th century fight for political and religious freedom. But God denies such freedoms. The Bible prescribes death penalty for any one who dares suggest a change of religious belief. What could be more cruel than what we read in the 13th chapter of Deuteronomy? "If thy brother or thy son or thy daughter or thy wife of thy bosom entice thee secretly saying let us go and serve another God, thou shalt surely kill him or her,

Thou shall stone him with stones till he dies". Thus, worshippers of all gods other than Jehovah must be killed. This type of commandments are the root causes of most of the massacres taking place in the name of \religions.

There are some Christians who say that the New Testament is in favour of religious liberty and tolerance. The truth is that the New Testament is as intolerable as the old. In Galatians chapter 1, verse 9, St. Paul declares. "If any man preach any other gospel unto you than ye have received, let him be accursed". Jesus the so called son of God says in St. Luke chapter 19, "But those mine enemies, which would not, that I should reign far over them, bring hither and slay them before me". In Mark, he says, "He that believeth and is baptised shall be saved, others shall be damned". Down the ages, Christians brutalised the intellectuals supported by biblical commandments. The church was eager to save the souls of men; but there was no salvation except for the docile believers. The duty of the church was to force all men to believe. It was an act of mercy to torture the body of the unbeliever in the hope of saving his soul hereafter.

## PERSECUTION

No power of imagination can conceive of the pain that has been inflicted on innocent men and women because the Bible is a persecuting book, and because, there fore, Christianity has ever been a persecuting faith. For ages Christians exhausted their ingenuity in devising ways and means of torture. Bible was their guide to torture. Following the teaching of the Bible has led to the massacre of millions.

## CANNIBALISM

What can be more revolting to civilised men than cannibalism? Though the savages of Africa and Pacific islands of dark ages ate the flesh of their enemies, killed in their tribal warfare, God-inspired Bible recommended eating the flesh of one's loved ones. In the 28th chapter of Deuteronomy it is said, "And thou shalt eat the flesh of thy sons and daughters. The flesh of children, the tender and delicate women among you". In the book of Jeremiah chapter 19, it is said, "And I will cause them to eat the flesh of their sons and the flesh of their daughters, and they shall eat every one, the flesh of his friend" The same horrible thing is again repeated in the book of Leviticus in chapter 26.

## MASSACRE OF THE INNOCENTS

Nothing could be more wicked than the fiendish command of Jehovah in the 15th chapter of the 1st Samuel, "Now go and smite Amalek, and utterly destroy all that they have, slay both men and women, infant and suckling, ox and sheep, camel and ass" In Deuteronomy chapter 20, God commands, "Thou shalt save alive nothing that breatheth".

If it is moral for Jehovah to order the destruction of all living things in Canaan indiscriminately, how can we blame die Americans, who worship the same God, for killing all living beings in Hiroshima and Nagasaki, or for adopting chemical warfare in Viet Nam?

Christian God's method of punishing the wrong-doers is by killing their infant children, and allowing their wives to be ravished by others. In 2nd Samuel chapter 12, God says, "I will raise up evil against thee out of thine own house, and I will take thy wife before thine eyes and give her unto thy neighbour and he shall lie With thy wife to thy presence and of all Israel". Worse still, if there can be anything worse, is God's command to parents to murder their stubborn children. In Deuteronomy chapter 21, the law stipulates, "If a man has a stubborn and rebellious son, who will not obey the voice of his father, or the voice of his mother, then shall his father and his mother lay hold on him, and bring him out unto the elders of the city, and they shall say, this son is stubborn and rebellious, and all the men of his city shall stone him with stones till he dies."

## PORNOGRAPHY AND SEX PERVERSION

No literature in the world can be worse than the Holy Bible for pornography and sex immorality. According to Jesus Christ it is moral to cohabit with one's brother's widow if she has no children. In Mark chapter 12 we read, "If a man's brother dies and leaves a widow behind him, and leaves no child, his brother should take the widow, and raise up sees unto his brother"

Although the Jews are strict adherent of the Old Testament, it is indeed a healthy sign that the present day Jews of Israel are able to see the immoral aspect of Jehovah's commandments. In January 1972, a 41-year-old-Israeli, Nissin Sharabi, was jailed in Tel Aviv for marrying Rivaka, the childless widow of his brother, in strict obedience to Jehovah's command.

Though God was in favour of a person cohabitting with his brother's widow, he did not favour parents giving their daughters in marriage. In 1st Corinthians chapter 7, God says, "He that giveth his own virgin daughter in marriage doeth well, but, he that giveth her not in marriage doeth better".

When Onan was compelled to cohabit with his brother's widow, he was reluctant to give birth to an illegitimate child. So he practised coitus interruptus. God therefore killed him not for his incestual act, but for his act of withdrawal. In chapter 7 of 1st Corinthians God commands, "If any man thinketh that he behaveth unseemly towards his virgin daughter, if she be past the flower of her age, let him satisfy his need. He sinneth not". Should we try to spread incest in the country by teaching Bible in our schools?

God encouraged prostitution and adultery. In Horsea chapter 4, God tells his chosen people, "I will not punish your daughters when they commit whoredom, nor your wives when they commit adultery".

While indecent exposure in public is a punishable offence in civilised countries, God's method of punishing women was to make her stand naked before the public! In Isiah chapter 3, it is said, "And the Lord will lay bare their secret parts".

According to Jehovah who created the women as the result of a second thought, women are mere chattels meant for the sexual gratification of men, and to be discarded if and when they cease to give them enough satisfaction. In Deuteronomy chapter 21, God commands, "And seest thou among the captives a beautiful woman, and if thou has a desire unto her, you would take her to thee as wife, thou shalt bring her home, and after that go unto her, and be her husband, and she shall be thy wife. And it shall be that of thou have no delight in her, then thou shalt let her go wither she will".

In all the aggressive wars waged by the Israelites against the inhabitants of Canaan, God insisted that they brought all the virgins alive, and gave him also a share. In Numbers chapter 31, God commands, "Now therefore kill every male among the little ones, and kill every woman that hath known man by lying with him, save all the virgins and keep them alive for yourselves". The Israelites strictly acted according to God's instruction. They brought back thirtytwo thousand virgins, and gave 32 of them as a tribute to their God. Thus God's tribute in virgin women was one per thousand! In sexual perversion the Christian God is not second to Hindu Gods! Like God Krishna, who was peeping from the top of a tree at Gopi women who were bathing in a pond, Jehovah also seem to be fond of feasting his eyes on the nude figure of his own creatures! In 2nd Samuel chapter 6, we read about King David, the man after God's own heart, performing a naked dance before women, just to please Jehovah!

## GENOCIDE

Hitler's persecution and mass massacre of the Jews, and Yahya Khan's genocide in East Pakistan pale into insignificance when compared with the atrocities and genocides committed by Jehovah against the Egyptians and the Canaanites. Even when Pharoah was willing to send away the Israelites, God made Pharoah's heart hard to change his mind, not once but several times. Why did this so-called merciful God do such a treacherous act? Just to find an excuse to kill more and more innocent women and children, and even their domestic animals? What crime these animals did do?

If there was a war crime tribunal during Biblical days, civilised man would have convicted the God of the Bible as the worst criminal the world had ever seen. If the Deluge story in the book of Genesis is true, it would make Jehovah guilty of the very worst crime ever committed. Why did he destroy all the innocent men, women and children who had not sinned against him?

Why did he destroy all the animals and vegetable lives on earth? What possible harm could have they done against him? He blamed everyone and everything for his own failures.

Can any civilised society allow their children to be taught in schools to hate their parents, their brothers and sisters or to create discord in their families? Are we to teach them peaceful ways or violence? In Mathew chapter 10, Jesus Christ says, "I came not to send peace, but sword. I came to set a man against his father, a daughter against her mother, and the daughter-in-law against her mother-in-law". In St. Luke chapter 22, Jesus advises his disciples to sell their cloaks and buy swords.

Teaching Bible in our schools, being extremely dangerous, should be banned by the state. If allowed, it might make our youths grow up into murderers, rapists, cannibals and immoral fellows of the worst type.

While civilised man is abolishing capital punishment, "eye for an eye" is the law of God. In 2nd King chapter 19, we read, "And it came to pass that night the Angel of the Lord went forth and smote the Assyrians an hundred fourscore and five thousand, and in the morning they were all dead corpses". If Jesus Christ could kill a fig tree for no fault of it, what kind of Justice man can expect from him or his father Jehovah? Who can be more wicked than a God who takes pleasure in human and animal sacrifices?

## SEAT OF EVIL

Why should the Satan or the Devil be blamed for evil in this world, when God himself accepts that he is the creator of evil? In Isaiah chapter 45, God says, "I form the light and create darkness. I make peace and create evil."

According to the well-known Bibliologist Marshall J. Gauvin, no other book in the world has such perverting influence on man than the so-called Holy Bible. Lying, cheating, stealing, slavery, murder, cannibalism, genocide, incest, prostitution, adultery, nudism, pornography, sexual permissiveness, tyranny and torture are some of the crimes the Bible sanctions and defends.

A reformist Christian priest once confessed to me that he has to waste a lot of time on Saturdays searching through the Bible to select suitable passages, free from obsene, immoral and unethical teachings to be read in his church at Sunday Services!

Considered as a moral guide, Bible is the most dangerous book in the world. There is no easier way to get into prison than by following the teachings of this inspired religious book. A perverted book of this nature should be kept away from the reach of our youth. Those Christian apologists who clamour for the teaching of Bible in our schools should read their Bible themselves before they press their demand

Chapter 12

## *MIRACLES AT LOURDES*

Every lay-member of the Roman Catholic Church, who is encouraged by the Church to go on pilgrimage to Lourdes, should read the book 'ELEVEN LOURDES MIRACLES' by Dr. D. J. West, M.B.CH.B., D.P.M. (Duckworth).

Dr. West critically examines the eleven cases that have been proclaimed miraculous by Canonical Commissions dating between 1937 and 1952. Each case has passed through the three stages necessary for adoption as miracles. They have been investigated and reviewed by the Lourdes Medical Bureau, by the International Medical Commission in Paris, and finally by the Ecclesiastical Commission. Any one of these three bodies may reject a case, and it is interesting to see how many are rejected.

In the years 1946, '47 and '48, the Lourdes Medical Bureau found 194 cases worthy of further examination, and eventually only 19 of the cases were passed on to the International Medical Commission. The Medical Commission accepted only one of these. In 1949 they accepted three and rejected three. Of the six cases accepted by the International Medical Commission only three have been declared by the Ecclesiastical Commission.

It will be seen then, that the Church does not rashly pronounce a miracle cure. Dr. West takes the eleven cures pronounced miraculous by the Canonical Commission since 1946. But he first makes clear the restricted nature of the miracles. They are not, he says, "of a type that an outsider would consider self-evidently miraculous. There are no cases of lost eyes or amputated legs sprouting anew. There are very few cases of recovery from incurable diseases, and very many cases of dramatically swift recovery from serious but potentially curable conditions like tuberculosis." He adds: "In most cases no claim can fairly be made about the cure unless the patient is subjected to rigorous examination immediately before and immediately after the alleged cure. Unfortunately, this never happens."

One of the eleven cases is considered in detail. It is that of Miss G. Clauzel, whose rheumatic spondylitis with compression of the nerve roots was allegedly cured during Mass on August 15th, 1943. The patient's own doctor (Dr. Maurin) provides the chief medical document dated May 21st, 1944, and this is given in full. Dr. West finds that: "As a medical document, Dr. Maurin's report, like so many of the accounts to be found in the Lourdes files and publications, is curiously imprecise and unsatis factory. Miss Clauzel had an obscure disorder of many years' duration, and at no stage does she appear to have had a complete investigation such as would be carried out on a similar case in any modern hospital."

The fact that the consultant referred to was a psychiatrist is withheld. "Dr. Maurin's explanation of the whole case in terms of extensive nerve-root compression is scarce- plausible." Miss Clauzel's symptoms seem to be more severe and extraordinary than can be accounted for by the spinal arthritis and postural defect which is all that is indicated in the X-ray report dated August 20th 1945. Dr. West suspects hysteria, and 'if the Clauzel case is just another example of hysteria cured dramatically by suggestion, it hardly seems worthwhile discussing it further.'

The Lourdes Medical Bureau's report throws no further light on the nature of the illness, but it reveals "an attitude of mind in the doctors responsible, who seem determined to avoid the obvious natural explanation."

The report of the Canonical Commission is also given, but it merely reiterates their own particular interpretation of the evidence "with no consideration of alternative possibilities", and it glosses over "the absence of any clear evidence as to the organic basis of Miss Clauzel's illness."

Dr. West concludes that "in this and in many other instances the Lourdes Bureau has lent its support to cures without sufficiently investigating the case, and without giving fair consideration to interpretations that do not fit in with the idea of a miracle."

The other cases are no more rewarding for the miracle seeker. Mrs. Costas (1947) has "such obvious possibilities for ordinary explanations". Even if Francis Pascal had been miraculously cured of his blindness in 1938.. "the medical documentation is so poor that we could never be sure of it".

Colonel Pellagrin's case of liver abscess and fistula (1950) is not remarkable for the healing, but for the "coincidence between the closure of the fistula and the visit to Lourdes", and the alleged rapidity of the healing. There is, also "impreciseness regarding crucial dates" and "as a result of treatment the Colonel's fever was cured, his general health improved and his weight increased long before he visited Lourdes. The closare of the fistula was merely the last stage of a lengthy process of recovery".

Sister Mary Marguerite did not go to Lourdes, but recovered after prayer and the taking of Lourde's water. "Without careful medical substanciation of such a case the sceptically minded are unlikely to be interested", says Dr. West, and "the original dossier has disappeared from the Lourdes files". In the report of the Lourdes Bulletin No. 69, July 1946, "we are told practically nothing" and the nun's medical adviser, Dr. philouze, reveals "a surprising lack of appreciation of the sort of information required so that one cannot place much confidence in his medical judgement".

Miss Cannin was said to be suffering from tubercular peritonitis when cured in 1947, but Dr. West protests against the view that T.B. Peritonitis was "finally established on clinical grounds". All that one can say is that the "patient suffered from a long-standing but fluctuating abdominal disturbance of undetermined origin". "It could have been in part, functional", he continues, for she "had recovered several times before and she recovered again very rapidly after her visit to Lourdes".

"Such an event", he says, "deserves no special comment".

Jeanne Fretel's case (1948) "seems practically most remarkable; it is a tragedy that information is so lacking. On the unsatisfactory, jumbled and inconsistent information available, no definite scientific statement can be made about Jeanne Fretel's condition".

The absence of 'crucial evidence' is 'regrettable' about Frauelin Traute Fulda (1950).

Regarding Mrs. Cauteault (1952); "since the underlying cause is so obscure, the diagnosis is more of a label than an exact scientific concept, and it may well cover a while a variety of philosophical processes".

In the case of Miss Louise Jamain (1937) Dr. West concludes "It is sad and tantalising that there should be conflict between the bacteriological and radiological findings, and consequent doubt as to the interpretation of the case".

Mrs. Rose Martin's (1947) case deserves clear scrutiny because it is claimed that she was cured of cancer. She had a swelling in the bowel which was diagnosed as cancer, but Dr. West finds it "surprising" that her surgeon (Dr. Fey) "did not consider it worthwhile to make sure the swelling was cancerous by ordering a biopsy or at least by carrying out a rectoscopy". Dr. Strobino at Lourdes argues that the diagnosis of cancer was virtually certain and a' biopsy was unnecessary since the patient was bedridden and wasting away; but this argument carries little conviction, says Dr. West, because "other complications besides cancer could have produced both swelling and wasting illness". Several examples are given, but the most likely is that Mrs. Martin was simply suffering from severe constipation and that the lump was "a mass of compressed faeces". It is known that she was taking large doses of morphine—a drug which causes severe constipation—and it is significant that the Lourdes doctors stressed that there had been "no abnormal evacuation of the bowels prior to the dramatic recovery". If there had been, says Dr. West, "it could have been an important point in favour of the compressed faeces or inflammatory mass interpretations, hence the importance of denying it". "Unfortunately for the protagonists of the miracle cure', he continues, "the Lourdes dossier contains an account by Mrs. Martin herself" of just such an evacuation during the journey. A nurse, Miss Glory, remembers that Mrs. Martin herself used the bed-pan, and that she was constantly demandmg morphine. On the advice of the pilgrimage doctor, Miss Glory, gave an injection of Lourdes water and camphor instead of the morphine—a fact that "may well explain the sudden relief of the patient's constipation, and passing away of the offending matter and consequent recovery". Dr. West doubts Mrs. Martin's cancerous condition and "therefore fails to see why her recovery was considered miraculous or even partially remarkable".

Each of the eleven cases mentioned in this book is found wanting. Insufficient evidence, unsatisfactory diagnosis, sometimes a lack of honesty; these and other factors help to create the illusion of Lourdes!

The weakness of the Lourdes doctors, says Dr. West, "is that, being impelled to arrive at a predetermined goal, they cannot let themselves be carried along by the facts, and must strive to carry the facts with them."

Dr. West is unlikely to convince a fervent Catholic, but he cannot fail to impress the critical reader. While the Lourdes Medical Bureau claims eleven miraculous cures during the years 1937 to 1952, no mention is made of the hundreds of deaths—miraculous or otherwise—which have taken place at Lourdes during the same period!

## Chapter 13

## *THE FLAMING FOREST OF OLUMADU*

We reached Mankulam Rest House at about 3 p.m. on Saturday in 1930. Others in my company on this Safari to Odduchuddan on the Mankulam-Mullaittivu road were Messrs. Samuel Jacob and S. A. Mann, both fellow teachers with me at Jaffna Central College.

With mugs of stout before us, we were finalising our plans for the shooting expedition that night. Chinnaiah, the local shikari and guide who was hired to accompany us, knew every nook and corner of the forest in that area.

He was engaged in showing us on a survey map spread on the large table some of the famous spots in that jungle where game could be had in plenty. The best among them, according to Chinnaiah, was a water-hole in the forest about a mile from Glumadu, a hamlet some three miles from Mankulam on the Muilaittivu road.

### KAADERI

Being the nearest and the most suitable place among the whole lot, all three of us decided to make the water-hole near Olumadu the venue of our hunt that night.

"We can't go there", said Chinnaiah with an air of authority. "It is true that there are a lot of animals there, but nobody can shoot even one of them. That area is protected by a ghost of 'Kaaderi' (a type of evil spirit haunting forests), and any one who trespasses the area is doomed."

"It is said that some six years ago, a party of four persons from Point Pedro who had gone on a shooting expedition to that waterhole were found dead with their guns by their sides. Had they taken with them a local guide, they would have been living today. None from this area would have taken them to this dangerous spot."

"The abode of the 'Kaaderi' and his wife", Chinnaiah continued, "are two 'palu' trees (Mimusops Hexandra)

Their children have taken abode in the neighbouring trees. People who have ventured to go near the waterhole with special protective charms have seen those flaming trees at night. During the day these spirits roam about in the forest in the form of wild animals. If anyone shoots one of them by mistake, it is not the animal which dies but the marksman. Many a hunter who had trespassed this area had to pay the penalty with his life."

"There is no day and night at this place. Because of the light emanating from the flaming trees on which the Kaaderi and family live, the whole place is bright like day, even at night."

## EXODUS

After listening to this eerie story, Jacob and Mann persuaded me to give up the idea of going to this haunted forest. Instead, they decided to go to a waterhole in the Oddichuddan forest.

As a result of intensive pleading and coaxing, Chinnaiah agreed to give me a chance of seeing, at least from a distance those 'Kaaderi'—haunted trees of the Olumadu forest, on condition that we entered the forest leaving our guns behind.

He insisted that all of us tied pieces of turmeric round our wrists to safeguard ourselves against the harmful influences of the 'Kaaderi' spirits.

We started by car from the Rest House after dinner at about 9 p.m. armed with guns, torches, field glass, knife, rope etc. Chinnaiah himself tied the charmed pieces of turmeric on our wrists.

After driving for about thirty minutes we stopped near a culvert, at Chinnaiah's instruction. He did not allow us to take the guns out of the car. Before entering the forest he made sure that the pieces of turmeric were intact on our wrists. He, too, had one on his Chinnaiah led the way with his special type of torch belted to his forehead, and the electrodes leading to dry batteries in his pocket. After walking for about a mile through the leech-infested forest whose gloomy hush was broken only by the shrill chirping of the Cicada and the occasional blood-curdling cry of the Devil bird, we came to a small open space. We were asked to stop there and look at the glowing trees about a hundred yards away.

## FLAMING TREES

Yes! What Chinnaiah said was perfectly true. There were about thirty of them—tall trees with their trunks shining like glowing embers. I looked through the field-glass, and what I saw was a marvellous sight never to be forgotten in my life. Two trees among the whole lot were so bright that their leafless branches also could be discerned.

"Those two trees are the ones which were originally possessed by the 'kaaderi' parents. As years go by, they are getting more and more children, and these children now live on the neighbouring trees. They do not allow any one to go near them even during the day", said Chinnaiah.

Though I wanted to go near to have a clear view, neither Chinnaiah nor my colleagues would allow me to place even one step forward. We returned to the car and drove off to Odduchuddan. All our efforts till 3 a.m. resulted in bagging only one wild boar and a rabbit.

We came back to the Mankulam Rest House before daybreak. As Jacob and Mann were keen on reaching Jaffna before the carcasses started decomposing, they wanted to start the return trip immediately. But I succeeded in persuading them to start after breakfast.

## REVISIT

By daybreak Mann, Chinnaiah and myself jumped into the car and proceeded to Olumadu to have a day-light look at the flaming trees. We reached the spot at 7 a.m. but we failed to identify the flaming trees we had seen the previous night. Disregarding Chinnaiah's violent protests, we went very close to the 'palu' trees and examined them.

There were two old trees, one dead and fully dried up and the other partially dead. The southern sides of most of the trees in the locality were slightly yellowish in colour. This yellow stain was more prominent in the two dead ones.

With the help of a knife I removed some bark and wood from the dead tree and took them with me to the car, and returned to the Rest House just in time for breakfast.

After reaching Jaffna, Jacob and Mann got busy with the two carcasses, while I was busy examining the bark and wood I had brought from Olumadu.

## FUNGUS

It was an interesting experience for my wife and the 3-year-old son that night to watch the luminous glow coming from my study table when the lights were switched off. That light emanated from the specimens of bark and wood I kept on the table after examination.

''They are the grand-children of the 'Kaaderi' of Olumadu forest", remarked my wife humorously to my son.

Next day I took the specimens with me to the Botany laboratory at Jaffna Central College for further examination. Microscopical examinations revealed that the yellow colouration on the barks of the 'palu' trees was due to the growth of a bioluminous variety of fungus. It was seen that the mycelial threads of this saprophytic fungus had penetrated deep into the hark and wood of the dead 'palu' tree.

It is not at all a strange phenomenon to come across luminosity emanating from fungus-covered trees in forests. They are more common on decaying trees than on living ones. Outer layers of barks of old trees, being dead, serve as suitable hosts for the growth of these fungi. It can be scraped off from the tree and cultured on suitable media in the laboratory.

All types of fungi are not luminous. The luminous species, whether it is in a laboratory culture or growing on a tree in the forest, give out light at night. It has nothing to do with 'kaaderi' or any other ghost.

## BIOLUMINESCENCES

Like these fungi, there are many other plants and animals which give out light at night. They are called bioluminous organisms. Most of the bioluminous organisms live in the sea, hence they are not very familiar to most people.

Among the luminous organisms on land, the most common ones are the 'glow-worms'. Others can be seen in thick forests and dark caves. The 'glow-worm' is a beetle, and not a worm. It is only the male 'glow-worm' that is capable of flight. The female remains on the ground or attached to some plants. The sexes are attracted to each other by their glows.

There are also numerous bacteria which can emit light. Decomposing proteins (meat, fish etc.,) become luminous at night due to the growth of such bacteria on them.

The interior of certain caves in New Zealand are said to become brightly lit due to the presence of a type of luminous worms in large numbers on their walls. Some worms have luminous spots on their heads. At night, when they move about they resemble slow-moving cars with their head-lamps switched on. The presence of a miscropical organism called Noctiluca causes the waters of tropical seas to glow when disturbed. Collection of large numbers of Noctiluca on the surface water of the sea in certain areas make the water there appear to be on fire. Just like the forest dwellers consider the glowing trees to be haunted, seafarers consider the glowing waters of certain parts of the sea to be haunted by some sort of aquatic ghost.

## PHOSPHORESCENCE

Like bioluminous organisms, certain types of pearls, cockle shells, fish, snails, centipedes, millipedes etc., become phosphorescent in the dark, especially when disturbed Raphael Duboi (1887) conducted researches on the light emission of Pholas shells and proved that the luminosity of those and similar ones was caused by the presence of a substance called 'luciferin.'

Luminosity of certain bacteria and fungi is continuous, whereas the glow of certain marine animals, like that of the glow-worm, is controlled by the nervous system of the animal concerned, hence not continuous. Bioluminescence and phosphorescence occur without production of heat. Luminosity varies in their intensity and colours. Green, blue, yellow and red are the usual colours of such lights. Some deep-sea-fishes have the power of varying the intensity of their lights.

## NOT MYSTERIOUS

There is nothing mysterious in the auto-luminescence of these organisms. The 'palu' trees of Olumadu were not burning. The glow originated from the panus fungus which grew on the barks of those trees. Probably the fungus started to grow first on the dead tree. From that it spread gradually to the neighbouring trees due to the dispersal of their spores. Because of this infectious spreading, the villagers thought or interpreted that the 'kaaderi' family was growing in numbers year after year.

It is a psychological weakness in man to attach divine or demoniacal influence on any occurrence for which he has no explanation. As a result of such beliefs, exaggerated stories of strange happenings gain circulation. The stories about the numerous deaths at Olumadu forest are good examples of such exaggerations.

By exposing the truth about the superstitious beliefs about 'kaaderi', I am doing a great disservice to the fauna of those haunted forests. No more such places will oe self-imposed sanctuaries for them. Will I be considered by the 'Wild Life Protection Society' as their 'number One' enemy?

## Chapter 14

### *SPIRIT MEDIUM*

In 1941, the District Judge (of Jaffna) had a lengthy conversation with his dead wife and obtained a lot of valuable informations regarding his personal as well as his family affairs. The Judge was the late Mr. Simon Rodrigo of Panadura and the medium through which he spoke to the spirit of his dead wife was Mr. X of Manipay.

The thought about the departed loving wife was tormenting Mr. Rodrigo from the day of her death. Obsessed by this thought he began to get interested in books on spiritualism. It could be said without any exaggeration that most of the books on spiritualism belonging to the Jaffna Public Library could be found in those days, more often on his tables, both at home as well as in his chamber at the District Court, than on the shelves of the Public Library. It was Mr. Rodrigo's quest after books on spiritualism that brought him in closer contact with me because I too had a number of books on the subject in my private library. Both of us used to spend hours together discussing and debating the question of survival after death.

Mr. Rodrigo's readings on the subject were so intensive and extensive that he could at any time quote, without actual reference, from such authors on spiritualism as Myers, Soal, Sidgwick, Podmore, Oliver Lodge, Alexander Cannon, Harry Price, Thouless and others just as a Jehovah's Witness could quote chapter and verse from any of the *66* books of the Bible. Though a Buddhist by birth and faith, Mr. Rodrigo found it easy to discard the doctrine of 'anatmas' in favour of the existence of the immortal soul as propounded in those books on spiritualism by their Christian authors.

JUBILANT

On 5th November, 1941, Mr. Rodrigo rushed into my house in an exceptionally jubilant mood and shouted, "Abraham! at last I managed to get my wife to talk to me! She spoke for about one hour and told me a lot of things she missed telling me before her death. I have fixed up another appointment with her for next Sunday, when I hope to ask her about many more things I want to know." He expressed these words with great difficulty as he was visibly moved with emotion. Tears flowed down his cheeks.

After a few minutes of silence and a cup of hot coffee,. Mr. Rodrigo regained his composure to resume his talk. He described how he met Mr. X of Manipay, who had developed the power of becoming a 'spirit medium' and how he spoke to his wife's spirit through him (Mr. X). When I expressed a wish to be present with him at the next seance, Mr. Rodrigo said that he liked to be alone with his wife next time as he had to get from her some information of a confidential nature.

MEDIUM

Mr. X paid me a visit on November 22nd, 1941 in response to a written request. As I came forward to greet my psychic visitor, Mr. X said, "From a distance I saw a halo round your head. I have heard from Mr. Rodrigo that you are a good student of spiritualism and are interested in 'astral beings'. Is that so?" I took the role of a listener and allowed Mr. X to continue his talk. That talk enabled me to form an opinion about him.

Mr. X was a member of a well-to-do family, brought up in a Christian atmosphere by religious parents. He was educated in a Christian school in Jaffna, and there he came under the influence of a European missionary pedagogue. Being educated and wealthy, he led a respectable life. He was well-connected in society, and maintained his dignity to suit his social status. He had no need to practice fraud to make a living. He was of pious disposition. When he was young, he had a desire to become a Christian priest, but gave up that idea when a brother of his took up that vocation.

He was devoted to his first wife who died in 1926 after giving birth to a daughter. Though he married a second time, the thought of his first wife was dominant in his mind. Like Mr. Rodrigo, Mr. X got interested in spiritualism after the death of his first wife. He became a member of the Society for Psychical Research (London), and was a regular reader of the Journal of that Society. He had with him the photographs of his father-in-law and wife taken many years after their death, by a spirit photographer in England. Though he doubted the authenticity of those photographs, he treasured them and kept them safely in his wallet, ready to be pulled out and shown to others when opportunities came. The blurred pictures in them, according to him, did not resemble the two persons concerned.

The first communication he had with his wife's spirit was in 1934. Since then he had communications with her on several occasions. He consulted her in all his important affairs. Though there was a high percentage of errors in messages he obtained from her, a few she said were marvellously correct. The marriage of his first daughter was conducted after consulting the spirit of his first wife. He said that he had developed his psychic powers to such an extent that he could communicate with her at any time and in any place.

## SEANCE

At this stage I requested him to get into communication with his wife's spirit. As he wanted a quiet place for the purpose, he was led into my library and made to sit on a chair. At his request, all the windows were closed. After a couple of minutes' stare on the opposite wall he lapsed into a trance. "Yes, now I can see my wife clearly. There! there she is standing, looking at me", shouted Mr. X pointing to a life-size portrait of The Verv Rev. Kovoor Eipe Thomma Kattanar, Vicar General of St. Thomas Syrian Church of Malabar, hanging on the wall.

"Can you see that photo hanging on that wall?" I asked. "There is no wall there. I can just see the blue sky with my wife standing among the clouds", said Mr. X. I walked upto the wall, touched the portrait of my late father and asked whether that was his wife. "Yes, that is she, but don't try to touch her. She is sure to disappear if you attempt to touch her with your mortal hands", said Mr. X. He then told me that his wife's spirit was ready to answer any questions. To the numerous questions of mine, he himself gave the following answers purporting to be coming from the spirit.

## ORACLE

"Christianity is the true religion. There is no rebirth or re-incarnation. Spirits have no knowledge of any life before they are born on this earth. There is food and drink in the spirit world. Spirits form small groups under separate leaders. They have to get special permission from their leaders to converse with mortals. There is sex for spirits. My wife wishes to lead a husband and wife life after my death. Spirits dress themselves in white flowing gowns. There are no spirits for baser animals. There are human beings in other planets. Spirits maintain the same body as they did when they were on this earth. From the spirit world they go to a higher plane of life, and finally they go to the God's world. There is whisky and soda in the spirit world. English is the language spoken by all the spirits."

Both myself and Mr. X came out of the library room after the seance and continued our talk in the living room. Asked about his experience just before, during and just after the seance, Mr. X said that when he sits concentrating his thoughts on his wife, he begins to see strange lights and figures before him. It was not necessary for her to 'materialise' to hold a conversation with her. He has held conversation with spirits other than his wife's. At the end of a seance he generally felt exhausted, thirsty and sleepy.

## PSYCHOPATH

All these alleged paranormal experiences of a psychopath like Mr. X are explicable in the light of modem psychology. There need not be any reality in the subjective experiences of such a person. Both Mr. Rodrigo and Mr. X were obsessed with the thoughts about their dead wives. Their constant readings about spiritualism and spirit materialisation have helped to confirm their belief in the existence of spirits and the possibility of holding conversations with them. On the other hand, had they been reading about the negative findings of the present-day members of the society for Psychical Research, like Antony Flew, Cutner, Simons, Edward Roux, Hansel, McCall, Spencer Brown and others, these two gentlemen would not have wasted their time chasing the non-existing spirits of their wives.

Though normal in other respects, Mr. Rodrigo and Mr. X were psychopaths only in relation to the subject of their obsession, viz., spiritualism. Both became monomaniacs as regards spiritualism was concerned. It is possible for maniacal obsession to develop in neurotic persons on diverse types of subjects. Most of the phobias and philoes originate that way. That Mr. X was a victim of severe hallucinations could be seen by his seeing strange lights and figures in space, and a halo round the head of an ordinary person like me. His illusionary mind made him see his wife in the portrait of my father. He could see neither the wall nor the portrait. His illusion was so strong that the wall changed into a blue sky, and the large portrait into his wife's astral body.

## ANALYSIS

All Mr. X said during the seance, allegedly coming from his wife's spirit were mere projections of his own ideas conditioned by his Christian beliefs and upbringing. Even the idea of food and drink in the spirit world might have originated in his mind from the gospel story of Jesus Christ, though no more a mortal after his resurrection, appearing before the disciples asking for food and eating it.

If the spirits too need food and drink, we have to conclude that they also are mortals. Since whisky and soda are available in the spirit world, there is scope for some of our people to continue their 'kasippu' industry even after their death as a market for their produce is assured in the summerland.

It was his Christian conditioning which made Mr. X say that there are no spirits for baser animals. Had he been a Hindu he would have conceded spirits even to bacteria. Mr. X's desire to lead a wife and husband life after the death of Mr. X was purely a wishful desire on the part of Mr. X. Probably he might have forgotten the fact that his monogamous matrimony on earth would have to end up in bigamy for ever after the death of his second wife.

Regarding' the spirit photographs of Mr. X's wife and father-in-law he, like many others in the past, was cheated by one of the many professional fake-photographers in England. Fred Barlow and Major Rampling Rose, joint authors of "Report on Investigations on Spirit Photography" have dealt in detail with the fraudulent techniques adopted *by* professionals in producing spirit photographs.

The idea that the departed souls maintain their earthly bodies, is in complete harmony with Mr. X's other foolish ideas such as food, sex, language, dress etc., pertaining to the spirits.

Are those bodies reconstituted from the separate elements after the decomposition of the corpses?

## Chapter 15

### *SANKILI VAIRAN OF MANDAITIVU*

Mandaitivu is a small islet to the south of Jaffna town separated from Peninsula by a lagoon. It is sparsely populated by a few farmers and fewer fisher folks. The main avocation of the farmers is tobacco cultivation. Though separated from the mainland by only about four miles of lagoon, most of its inhabitants remained cut off from the rest of the world. Most of them, especially women and children, looked forward to the annual festival at the Nallur Kandasamy Temple in Jaffna, for that was an yearly occasion for them to cross the lagoon by boat and see the 'splendours' of urban life.

With the main idea of collecting marine and halophytic specimens, I decided to spend the April holidays of 1932 in this islet. For our stay there I booked the only holiday-bungalow there which belonged to that well-known educationist the late Mr. Nevins Selvadurai. It was on the southern coast of the island facing the open sea. The shallow stretch of water between the shore and the distant coral reef served both as a bathing place and a hunting ground for marine specimens.

While I spent the forenoons in the sea with my wife and son. the afternoons were used for siesta followed by long walks to the various regions of the islet. During one of these evening walks, I came across a Vernacular school-teacher. He was the first person I saw in that islet wearing a shirt. Mr. Markandu—that was his name —introduced himself to me, and both of us had a long chat, mostly about the social life of the people of the place. From that day onwards Markandu made it a point to visit me at my temporary residence for a chitchat.

One evening Markandu appeared with a collection list. He said that the people of the hamlet were thinking of bringing a famous 'yogi' from the precinct of Nallur Temple to conduct a special 'yagna' to drive away an evil spirit which was haunting the hamlet for the last few weeks. This spirit has appearedto different people at different places in different forms.Some have seen it in the form of 'Sankili Vairan' andothers in the form of 'Mohini.'

## APPARITION

"One night when a woman got out to the back yard of her kitchen she was beckoned by a woman standing near a coconut palm", said Markandu, "She lost her memory and followed the woman to some distance, but all-of-a sudden the strange woman disappeared into thin air. It took about three hours for the woman to regain her memory; but from that day she started talking and behaving like a possessed person. On another occasion a young man who was returning from his tobacco farm late at night met a pretty young girl on the foot-path. She told him that she had lost her way, and requested him to escort her to her father's house. Both of them walked together a short distance talking to each other, but all-of-a-sudden he lost sight of her although he could still hear her talking to him. He got frightened and ran away home. Panting for breath, he got home fully exhausted, and fell into a deep swoon. He gained consciousness only the next morning."

"A 7-year-old girl saw a black dog in the court yard of her house one night. She threw a stone at that dog to chase it away. Thereupon the dog transformed into a 'Sankili Vairan' frightened that girl to such an extent that she lost her voice from that day."

## YOGI

"The elders of the hamlet held a conference last week and decided to bring the saintly 'yogi' from Nallur and conduct a 'yagna' to drive away the evil spirit from the island. This 'yogi', who is reputed to possess marvellous powers, spends only two months in the year at Nallur. The rest of the time he spends worshipping at Tiruketheeswaram, Kataragama and Sivanadi Padam (Adam's peak)".

I explained to Markandu my views on the subject, and refused to contribute even one cent towards the proposed attempt to drive away imaginary spirits; but I expressed my desire to witness the pooja if it was held before I left the island.

A week later Markandu came to the bungalow and informed me that elaborate preparations were being made to conduct the 'yagna' next Sunday, and that three persons have left for Jaffna by boat to bring the 'sacred' man.

That Sunday, after an early dinner, I went to a farmer's house where men, women and children from neighbouring houses had assembled to witness and take part in the pooja. Under a specially constructed canopy sat the venerable-looking bearded 'yogi' clad in a flowing yellow robe with three rows, of "Rudraksha" (Elaeocarpus) garlands hanging from the neck. His forehead was profusely smeared with holy ash. In front of him there were two brass lamps and numerous trays containing flowers, fruits, and various kinds of grains. To his right was a bronze saucepan supported on three stones with a few coconut shells under. Also there were five bottles containing five different kinds of oils such as ghee, coconut, gingelly, margosa and bassia oils.

## YAGNA

The pooja started with the yogi chanting manthras and slokas both in Sanskrit and Tamil. This went on for more than one hour. Chanting over, the yogi sat in meditation with closed eyes and wide open mouth with his tongue protruding. Yogi's assistant, who too had come all the way from Nallur, took a piece of camphor, lit it and placed it on the protruding tongue of the 'yogi'. A large tongue of flame, similar to a volcanic fire, was discharged from the yogi's mouth. Immediately he spat out the burning camphor into the bronze saucepan. Three times flaming pieces of camphor was introduced into the mouth of the 'yogi' amidst the shouting of 'hari-haro-hara' from the congregation.

After this the 'yogi' was seen lapsing into a deep meditation. He sat cross-legged holding the toes with his hands. He called Markandu, who was the only shirted man in the whole crowd barring me, and asked to feel his pulse at the wrist of his right-hand. A few seconds after Markandu started feeling the pulse he shouted, "Swami's pulse has stopped." The whole crowd shouted in unison, "hari-haro-hara' After Markandu, an elderly farmer went forward and felt the pulse of the 'yogi'. He too announced that the pulse of the 'yogi' had stopped. Immediately after this I took my turn to feel the yogi's pulse. To begin with it was beating normally, but gradually I felt the intensity going down, and finally it stopped completely. After about five minutes I began to feel the pulse-beat starting again and gradually regaining normal strength.

After this miraculous performance, the 'yogi' instructed his assistant to light the fire under the bronze saucepan. He poured the five kinds of oil into the saucepan and set fire to the coconut shells. When the oil started boiling, the 'yogi' took three lime fruits sanctified them by repeating some manthras, cut them and introduced into the oil. When the oil reached full boiling stage, the 'yogi' called all those persons who wanted to get immunised from the evil doings of the 'Sankili Vaian' to come forward one by one.

The oldest man in the congregation went forward first and knelt before the yogi. The mystic blew off the thick fumes emanating from the saucepan, and to the amazement of all who were there, he touched the surface of the boiling oil with the fingers of his right hand. He lifted up the hand quickly, and rubbed it vigorously against the left palm. Smeared a bit of the oil on the forehead of the old man and waved him to move off. In this fashion he anointed the foreheads of all the persons—men, women and children—who had assembled there with the sole exception of myself. With one dip of his hand in the boiling oil he managed to anoint about five or six persons. Although at the early stage he was dipping only the tip of his fingers, towards the later part he was seen dipping his whole palm in the boiling oil. It was really a stunning sight for all to witness, and during the whole proceedings the cry of 'hari-haro-hara' continued.

## EXORCISM

After this, the fire under the saucepan was extinguished. The 'yogi' then pulled out a highly polished coconut shell from a bag and kept it inverted in front of him. He also pulled out a small bottle of 'theertham' (holy water) ana 'seven small cowry shells. One of the cowries was kept at the vertex of the coconut-shell-dcme, and the rest were arranged round it. In a short speech he told the people, "I find that it is not one spirit that is haunting this place. There are seven of them, male and female, and all of them are equally powerful They are represented by these seven cowries I have kept on the top of this coconut shell. When I drop the "theertham" on them and recite a charm, those of the spirits which are prepared to get away from this island now, will indicate it by their cowries leaving this coconut shell and getting down on the ground. This coconut shell represents your island. Refusal of any cowry to move away from the dome is an indication that that spirit is not leaving tonight. In that case a more elaborate 'yagna' has to be done on a subsequent date."

The yogi then poured a few drops of the "theertham" from the bottle and recited the 'manthra'. To the surprise of all, the lifeless cowries showed signs of animation and started moving apart from each other, and finally slided down the sides of the dome. All the seven cowries were at last on the ground, and the yogi announced that all the evil spirits have left, the island for good.

At about 2 a.m. the whole ceremony was over. On behalf of the residents of the hamlet Markandu presented a purse to the 'yogi'. and made a short speech thanking him for getting rid of the evil spirits from their hamlet. Before leaving for Jaffna next day, the 'yogi' gave 'darshan' to many individuals and accepted their humble offerings in return for special blessings.

## SPIRITUAL POWERS

Next day Markandu came to me in a triumphant mood. "Now are you convinced about the spiritual powers of holy men. for which science has no explanations to give?", asked Markandu. "After seeing those cowries move unaided, will you now accept the existence of spirits, and that they have the power of setting material objects in motion? With your science can you dip your hands in boiling oil? Can you put burning camphor in your mouth? Who is the scientist in this world who can stop his pulse at will as Yogis do? You being a true investigator of paranormal happenings, I hope what you witnessed last night will make you change your opinions about spirits and the spiritual powers of mystics."

Answering my questions, Markandu said that the purse he presented the yogi contained five hundred and one rupee. I told him that.it was far too much for a few items of simple tricks performed in the name of 'yoga', one of the best systems of physical culture and auto-suggestive practice in the world. Though some imposters among yogis claim supernatural powers, there is nothing in a 'yogi' to be considered sacred or supernatural. I asked Markandu to bring with him next evening some of the elders who were responsible for organising the 'yagna', to witness a free show of all what the 'yogi' did.

My servant boy got busy next day removing the fibre from the basal half of. a coconut shell, and polishing it glass-smooth with sand-paper. I collected a few small cowry shells from the sea-beach and filed their bases flat and smooth. A packet of camphor and a few lime fruits also were procured. At about 5 p.m. next evening Markandu and five fanners arrived. I sat on the floor cross-legged in the fashion of the 'yogi'. A lighted candle was placed before me. A primus stove, with an aluminium saucepan on it containing some coconut oil and a. few cut limes, was placed to my right. Also there was a small bottle containing a clear liquid.

I started my so-called pooja first by lighting a piece of camphor and placing it on my outstretched tongue, The flame shot out from my open mouth for a few seconds, and. I spat out the burning camphor on to the floor. This I repeated three times like the 'yogi'. Then I asked Markandu to feel the pulse at my left wrist. To his amazement, I stopped my pulse for about five minutes. The five members also took their turn to feel my pulse stopping. They were fully convinced that my pulse too stopped like that of the 'yogi'.

During this time my servant boy was busy lighting the pressure stove. After a short while the oil started boiling, and while the pieces of lime were rolling about in the boiling oil I blew off the thick fumes from the surface and dipped my right palm in it, lifted it and rubbed it against the left. This I repeated several times. Lastly I took the polished coconut shell and kept it inverted before me. The seven cowries were arranged at the crown of the coconut shell in the fashion of a gold-smith setting precious stones on an ear-stud. When a few drops of the liquid from the small bottle were poured on the cowries, they started moving apart, and finally glided down the sides of the dome.

## SIMPLE TRICKS

For a short while my spectators remained spell-bound and silent. I explained to them that there was nothing mysterious either in what I have done or what the 'yogi' did two days ago. The liquid I poured on the cowries was lime juice. What the 'yogi' poured out from his bottle also must have been a dilute acid—probably vinegar or lime juice. Cowry, being a Calcium Carbonate, reacted with the citric acid present in the lime juice, and produced numerous bubbles filled with carbon dioxide. The pieces of cowries .were inconspicuously raised up from the coconut shell by the thousands of microscopic bubbles produced during the chemical reaction. The repeated formation and bursting of these bubbles made the cowries move down the sides of the dome due to gravitational pull.

The temperature of boiling oil is so high that it is not possible for any, one to dip the hand in it without suffering burns. But the temperature of boiling oil—whether it is one kind or a mixture of five kinds—as long as there is moisture in it, will not rise above 100 degrees centigrade if the saucepan is kept open. The cut pieces of lime which contains a lot of water, keeps the temperature of the boiling oil at 100 degrees centigrade. Even so, the temperature of the oil at its surface where water turns into vapour at a rapid rate, is liable to be lower. When the steam is blown off just before dipping the palm, a further lowering of temperature takes place on the surface instantaneously. No doubt the oil is still hot enough to be felt, and to some extent, to be painful, but not hot enough to burn or to cause blisters during a quick dip. The equally quick rubbing with the left palm reduces the pain. Had it not been for the presence of lime in the oil neither the 'yogi' nor myself could have touched the boiling oil without burning our palms.

Camphor is a highly volatile substance capable of turning into vapour without changing into liquid state. Because of its volatility it is highly inflamable. Just before placing the burning camphor on our wet tongue both the yogi' and myself wetted our lips with saliva and took deep breaths. Throughout the short time when the burning camphor was on our tongue we were continuously blowing out the flames at a stretch. The spitting out of the flaming camphor was completed before the end of the exhalation. If, by a mistake either of us had inhaled even for a split second, the result would have been disastrous.

## Chapter 16

### *CHARM CONTRA'CHARM*

Myself and my wife were spending the week-end with our friend Mr. M. C. Paul at his quarters at the Government Coir Factory at Kutunayake, of which he was then Manager. While at dinner we heard the faint throbbing of continuous drumming from a distance. "Ah! they have started the charm 'cutting' ceremony at Sirisena's house", said Mr. Paul.

Sirisena, a worker at the Coir Factory, became insane some seven months ago. The change in him appeared all of a sudden. He became violent and aggressive at times, but when he came to the factory he remained very weak and uncommunicative. Though mentally sick, Sirisena continued to go to the factory and draw his wages regularly.

One day Sirisena did not go to the factory for work. As usual he left home in the morning at 7 a.m. Till 6 p.m. that day Mary, his wife, was under the impression that her husband was at the factory. Next day Mary and all her relations searched in vain for Sirisena all over Katunayake.

A couple of days later Mary and her brother Premaratne decided to seek the help of a sooth-sayer of Jaela to find the whereabouts of Sirisena. Before day-break both of them were at the sooth-sayer's house. The sooth-sayer looked into the 'anjanameliya' and said that her husband would never come back as he has committed suicide by jumping into the sea.

Mary and her brother returned to Katunayake with heavy hearts. Her relatives kept constant vigil for many days along the sea-coast hoping to recover the corpse of Sirisena. Though they failed to recover the corpse, they did not fail to perform all the customary after-funeral rites, lest the ghost of Sirisena gave trouble to Mary and her two children.

## RETURN OF THE FUGITIVE

Six months later, one fine morning Sirisena was seen lying on the verandah of his own house. Mary's joy at her husband's resurrection disappeared gradually when she realised that his mental condition was worse than what it was before. It was not at all possible for anyone to find out from Sirisena where he had been during the last six months. He remained mum to all questions put to him.

At Premaratne's suggestion it was decided to consult a more powerful sooth-sayer this time to effect a radical cure for Sirisena's insanity. Mary and Premaratne went all the way to Nugegoda to consult a famous woman sooth-sayer in the neighbourhood. The usual offerings of money rolled up in betel leaves was made.

Mary and the sooth-sayer woman answered each other's questions to the best of their knowledge. Mary had to answer more questions than the sooth-sayer. Finally she looked into the 'anjanameliya' and said that Mary's husband was suffering as he was under the speil of a powerful charm by a Malayalee charmer. He was charmed at the instance of an enemy of Sirisena who was a fellow worker at the factory.

"This charm can be cut only by a more powerful Malayalee charmer", she said, "If you are prepared to pay his fee of Rs. 300, I can get the assistance of such a person."

Mary after a consultation with Premaratne agreed to the proposal and paid an advance of Rs. 30. It was finally agreed that the charm 'cutting' ceremony would be performed the following Saturday night.

## CHARM 'CUTTING'

Dinner over, Mr. Paul and myself were seated with others in the drawing room talking late into the night. We could still hear the distant drumming from the charm 'cutting' ceremony at Sirisena's house. I took part in the conversation mechanically while my thoughts were at the necromancist's ceremony. Not being able to resist my yearning to see charm 'cutting' ceremony I suggested that we walk upto the house where the ceremony was taking place.

The time was 11 p.m. Mr. Paul and myself got into our sarongs and banians and walked along the Negombo road a quarter of a mile and reached the house of Sirisena. They merged into the vast crowd in the courtyard where the ceremony was going on in full swing. A few in the crowd recognised Mr. Paul and made for him and me to take a ringside stand.

The charmer was seated cross-legged behind a brass lamp. More lights came from a dozen torches. A two yard square plot was marked off in the courtyard with white lines. At the four corners of this square there were new earthen pots holding coconut inflorescences.

Flowers of 'Araliya' and jasmine were strewn on the floor. In the centre a rooster with its legs tied up lay in a coma. There were numerous trays containing scarosant articles such as husked coconuts, paddy, puffed rice, plantains, Ixora flowers and a large conch shell.

## DIZZY DRUMMING

Amid frenzied drumming and blowing of conch shell the charmer accompanied by his two assistants kept on chanting from an old book kept open in front. Because of the defening noise of drumming none in the crowd could hear what they chanted. I moved and stood behind the charmer to get a clear view of things. From this vantage I could understand some of the words of their chant. It was a language familiar to me.

Since the ceremony started as early as 8 p.m., and the monotonous chanting went on for about four hours, most of their children and women who were seated on the ground were showing signs of fatigue. Sirisena who was made to sit on the outer border of the square facing the charmer was now prostrate on the ground in deep slumber, so also were some women and children.

The time was now close upon 1 a.m. The charmer and his two assistants stood up and performed a frenzied dance with occasional shrieking shouts and the blowing of the conch shell. Then all of a sudden the dancing and the drumming came to an abrupt stop. With an arecanut infloresence in the left hand and a torch in the right held high the cnarmer shouted, "The charm is buried 5 strides west of the house and 3 strides north of a plaintain tree."

All those who were sleeping, including Sirisena, got up.

## CHARM IS OUT

A procession headed by the charmer and followed by the drummers, the torch-bearers and the vast crowd, took me and Mr. Paul also to the rear garden of the house. The charmer measured five strides from the house by himself placing the distance and selected one of the many plantain trees in that line. He paced three more strides from the plantain tree northward and marked that spot.

A pooja was performed, and one of- the assistant was seen sprinkling some puffed rice at the spot. A spade was ordered to be brought. The crowd was asked to clear off. Except the charmer, his two assistants, the drummers and the torch-bearers, nobody was allowed within ten feet of the marked spot.

Sirisena was led into the arena and was made to sit on a stool. The charmer ordered one of his assistants to dig out the charm from the marked spot The digging started with renewed drumming and chanting. I warned my friend Mr. Paul not to take his eyes away from the digging operation whatever happened around

After a few minutes of futile digging in that place the charmer ordered his assistants to dig along two feet in the westerly direction. This too being futile, he was ordered to dig two feet in the north-easterly direction. As the charm could not be found there too he was ordered to dig along a south-easterly direction. Finally when that too failed, the .charmer ordered a pot of water to be poured in the original central spot. With the torch and the arecanut inflorescence in his hands the charmer walked round the spot three times, and ordered the central spot to be dug deeper.

## RITUAL IN THE DARK

As the person who was digging all this time showed signs of fatigue, the other assistant stepped in and started digging. While he was digging deeper and deeper, the drumming reached a crescendo, and all of a suddcn the charmer started dancing round Sirisena shouting incoherent words with the accompaniment of blowing of conch shell and ringing of a gong.

While the whole crowd was looking at the ecstatic dance of the charmer, myself and Mr. Paul had our eyes fixed to the spot where the digging operation was going on. Both of us saw something dropping on the ground from the folds of the sarong worn by the digger. As that object got buried immediately under the next spadeful of earth, we could not distinctly see what it really was.

About one minute later the charmer stopped his dancing and ordered the digger to stop. He called for the rooster. The other assistant held the cock, head in one hand and then tied-up legs in the other. It was not allowed to cry. While it was being held just above the central pit, a 'manthra' was chanted and the head of the innocent rooster was severed. The blood was drained into the pit. A lime fruit too was cut above this pit. The charmer said that further digging has to be done with washed hands.

## HOCUS-POCUS

Mary's brother Premaratne was asked to come forward. His hands were washed with the 'holy' water poured out by the charmer himself from a brass mug. He was asked to take out all the loose earth with his hands from the pit. While doing this he came across a cylindrical object similar to a plantain fruit about five inches long and two inches thick.

The charmer jumped up and took it from Premaratne's hands. After examining the exterior of it carefully he shouted, "This is the charm which was responsible for all the troubles in this house. It must have been buried here al least some eight months ago." He held it up and took it round for all in the crowd to see. It was blackish brown in colour with slight traces of blue patches here and there.

## THE TALISMAN IS FOUND

The charmer now sat cross-legged in front of Sirisena who now appeared to be a bit agitated. Failing his attempt to open the cylindrical object with his hands, the charmer called for a hammer or a chopping knife. Mary brought out a kitchen knife. After laborious efforts the charmer succeeded in opening it.

Among the items pulled out from the copper container there were some pieces of small bones, a human molar tooth, a small copper plate with some undecipherable writings, a lock of human hair, one copper coin of Travancore State known as 'chakram', and a beak of fowl. He examined all those things carefully and showed them to Sirisena, Premaratne and Mary. He put all those things back into the container, and said, "I will take this charm with me and destroy it. For the coming three days camphor must be burnt in this pit sharp at 6 p.m. At the same time I will be performing 'pooja' at home for three days."

The crowd dispersed to their homes fully convinced about the mysterious powers of the charmer both for charming as well as for cutting it. The charmer and his party, after collecting Rs. 270 from Premaratne, were looking around for a place to lay their heads to get a wink of sleep till day break. At my suggestion, Mr. Paul walked up to the charmer and said that he and his men could make use of a shed at the Coir Factory to sleep that night. They were happy to follow me and Mr. Paul to the factory for their much-needed rest.

While others in the party got into deep slumber soon after they lay down, the charmer had to remain awake talking to me and, my friend till 3 a.m. During the conversation which went on in Malayalam, I pretended to be one who knew all the tricks-of-the-trade in the field of charms. Among other things, I gathered the following information from him: —

The charmer and his two assistants were Malayalees. The others in the party were Sinhalese hired *for* the occasion at the rate of Rs. 5 per person per night. They were familiar with the routines connected with the charm 'cutting' ceremonies though they did not know the secrets involved.

Of the stipulated fee from the householder, 10 percent had to be given to the sooth-sayer who recommended them. They lived at Pannipitiya, and their normal avocation was growing grass for cattle fodder. Their chance for practising necromancy come only occasionally.

About twenty five copper cylinders of the type shown to the crowd that day, filled with objects like bones, hair, coins etc., are kept buried in the earth for a long time. Whenever they got a chance of going out to perform a charm 'cutting' ceremony, one of the cylinders is dug out and taken with them.

If the ceremony is conducted a few days after the 'call', and if the place is not far off, four of these cylinders are buried stealthily at four corners in the garden during one of the preceding nights.

A bucket of water was emptied into the pit before the charm was pulled out, to make the sandy earth of Katunayake cling on to the cylinder and thus obscure the black clay on it from the grass fields. Such precautions are more necessary if the earth in the garden happens to be red in colour.

The all-night chant came from the epic poem "Mary Magdalene" by the late Maha Kavi Vallothol of Kerala, the charmer learned in his school-days!

## *Chapter 17*

### *AN IMMACULATE CONCEPTION*

Mr. X is a retired Government servant. He retired on reaching his 60th year in 1962 as an Assistant Commissioner of an important department. He is a member of a well-known and well-to-do family, often in the social and political lime-light in Sri Lanka.

On 26th November, 1967, Mr. X came with his young wife to meet me. Leaving Mrs. X in the drawing room. Mr. X was taken upstairs to my study. He had a long story to tell me.

"Jerene is my second wife. She is from Matara. My first wife who was a sister of Mr. Y, our former Ambassador, died leaving a child. This child too died later. I married Jerene after I retired from service. We have now two children a three-year-old girl and an eleven-month-old boy.

"Two months ago on a rainy day, since there was nothing else to do, we indulged in a session of tumbler-talk. We had this type of fun on a previous occasion also. Alphabets from A to Z were written with a chalk in a circle on the dining table, and a tumbler was placed inverted in the centre. Both Jerene and myself placed our forefingers on the tumbler, and called for a spirit to come.

#### SPIRIT COMES

"After a few minutes of suspense the tumbler started to move slowly on its own accord. As time went on, the movement became faster and faster and the tumbler began to touch the letters. We jotted down on a paper the letters in the order in which the tumbler touched them so as to read the messages we received

"The first spirit which operated the tumbler was that of the late Prime Minister Mr. S. W. R. D. Bandaranaike. Since Mr. Bandaranaike was a friend of ours we asked him many questions, for which we got correct answers.

"The second spirit which moved the tumbler was that of one Thomas Silva, a person unknown to us. We did not ask him many questions. The third which appeared was that of the late Madam Boonwaat. She said that she was shot and killed by her own husband.

"The fourth spirit to appear was that of Mr. L. H. Methananda. Before Mr. Methananda's death both of us had worked together as members of a religious organisation. His spirit gave me a lot of information useful to me. The next spirit to appear was that of Mr. T. U. de Silva. As a leading member of a political party to which I too belonged, I was very friendly with him. The sixth spirit was that of Mr. C. T. Jayasundera, another family friend. He advised Jerene to take special care of my health.

"After lunch and siesta, we had a second session of the tumbler-talk. This time Vishnu was the first to appear. When we asked him certain questions, his counter question was why we were doubting his identity. The next to appear was the Kataragama Devio. He wanted us to make a pilgrimage to Kataragama within two months.

## ST. JUDE APPEARS

"The last spirit to appear was that of St. Jude. He asked me to give Jerene a gold ring as a present on his behalf. He also said that he would leave another gold ring for Jerene at the foot of his own statue in St. Anne's church. He wanted her to go there and light candles before the statue and collect the ring.

"Next day both of us went to St. Anne's church, and lighted candles before the statue of St. Jude, but there was no ring anywhere there. Jerene was thoroughly disappointed and upset. On our way back I told her that we should not indulge any more in calling these spirits home through tumbler-talks.

"But without my knowledge Jerene conducted a tumbler-talk alone that night. It seems St. Jude appeared again and told her that he was extremely sorry for not placing the promised ring at the foot of the statue. He said that he did so because I was with her at that time, and requested her to go to the church the next day without me.

"The next day she went to the church with her sick brother. There she prayed and lighted candles before the statue, yet the ring was not to be found. She waited there for a long time and prayed with tears in her eyes, only to be disappointed a second time. She refused to leave the church without the ring. Finally she had to be forcibly taken into the car by her brother and the driver.

## INSANE PERSON

"From the time she came back home she was behaving like an insane person, always talking about St Jude. During the last three weeks she is always crying and saying that she is expecting a baby. Although she says she is nine months pregnant, there is no visible sign of it. Moreover, since the birth of my second child we had no marital relationship. As I am now engaged in devotional meditation, I refrain from sex indulgence.

"During the last two months I have taken her to numerous places and persons to get a cure for her insanity Her brother took her to a reputed Roman Catholic church at Kochchikade. But she came back in a worse state.

"At the advice of some of our friends she was taken to another church at Nayakakande. Still there was no improvement. Then we consulted a soothsayer at Dematagoda. He said that Jerene's troubles were due to the 'dishti' of a female demon called 'Kalukumariya'. As a remedy he performed some poojas for a stipulated fee. Still there was no change in Jerene's condition. Then we consulted a Kattadiya of Pamankada. He said the trouble was caused by the spirit of my first wife. To ward off this spirit's influence, he gave some charmed oil, and also tied a charmed thread round her wrist These too proved futile.

"Later we took her to a famous soothsayer woman of Mirihana. When we were there she looked into anjanaeliya and gave a description of our house, and some of the things she said were right. She said that Jerene was given a special type of poison in 'Kaludodol' by an enemy of ours. She said that she could make Jerene vomit the poison. We agreed and made the special payment.

Jerene was given something to drink, and later she vomitted. But the trouble still continued.

"Then I took her to a Roman Catholic priest at Wattala. He said it was the work of satan. He sprinkled some Holy Water on her, and prayed touching her forehead with a cross. There was no cure.

"As instructed by the Kataragama Devio during the tumbler-talk, we took her to the Kataragama temple. There during the pooja she got into a trance. After our return she appeared to be normal, but the trouble started again after one day.

"Finally, three days ago we got down a party of Kattadiyas from Metale and conducted an all-night 'thovil'. During the 'thovil' Jerene danced with the Kattadiyas While she was dancing the Kattadiya asked her who she was. To this she replied that she was my first wife' and promised to leave Jerene's body by entering the body of a cock, which was later killed. She fell down in a faint and remained in that condition for more than an hour. In the morning Jerene appeared to be quite normal.

"I paid them their stipulated fee. When they were leaving, a young fellow in the party told me that if there was any relapse, I must try to contact you. Yesterday Jerene started to cry again and complain about her pregnancy."

## HISTORY

At this stage I asked Mr. X to go down and send his wife up. My wife brought Jerene and made her relax on the couch. While coming up she was seen muttering something inaudibly.

Jerene was dressed in a rich saree in a very modern style. Though 44, she looked much younger. A healthy specimen of a good-looking young lady with the complexion of ripe 'Kolikuttu' plantain. Though fashionable in appearance, she was meek and modest—the hall mark of a conservative upbringing.

Under light hypnosis she said, "My home is at Matara. I had my education at the Matara Convent. Though it was not compulsory for non-catholics to attend religious instruction classes, I used to join my Christian class mates in attending those classes and even their prayers. Both my husband and myself are Buddhists.

"Though this is my husband's second marriage, this is my first. We are a happy couple, loyal to each other. After my second child's birth we have decided to have no more children, because, if something happens to my husband I will not be' able to give them good education. My husband sleeps in a room close to the shrine room. I sleep with the children in another room.

"In the shrine room there is a statue of Lord Buddha with one of Vishnu and another of the Kataragama Devio on either side There is an oil lamp burning day and night in front of the statues. Flowers are offered daily.

"Financially we are well-off. My husband is a pious and religious person. We respect other religions also. On poya days we go regularly to the temple.

"When I conducted the tumbler-talk alone, St. Jude told me a lot of things, and asked me not to tell them to my husband. He told me that he loved me, and that I was his wife in my past birth. In my last birth my name was Rose, and his name Roily the Remus. He said that he wanted to be my husband in my next birth also.

"After the tumbler-talk session St. Jude used to come very often at night and sleep with me. Sometimes when my husband is away from home, he comes to the kitchen and drags me to the bathroom. There he used to embrace me and make love with me. Sometimes he removes my dress, and draws the sign of the cross on my body. Occasionally he bites me without giving much pain."

At this stage, without any hesitation she opened her blouse and showed us a scratch mark in the form of a cross on her chest, and a bite mark on the right hand.

She continued, "Since he is kind to me I like him very much. He is a very handsome person. He is entirely different from what we see in his, statue. He is clean shaved.

"One day he wrote on a paper that he would squeeze my neck if I told these things to my husband. On another occasion he removed the wedding ring and the pair of ear studs from me. On three occasions he left money under my pillow—Rs. 1000, Rs. 16000 and Rs. 800."

After saying these things, she started to cry bitterly. When I asked her why she was crying, she said, "I am expecting a baby. This is the 9th month. When the child is born next month, all people will know my husband is not the father. It is better for me to die than to give birth to an illegitimate child."

At this stage I woke her up, and my wife took her downstairs and Mr. X was asked to come up again.

## THE CAUSE

When Mr. X took his seat I gave him a copy of the Ceylon Observer (Sunday Edition) of January 12th 1964, in which there was a similar case I investigated at Padukka. It was about a school girl named Latha who had the hallucinatory experience of her dead lover's so-called spirit visiting her at night and making love with her.

When Mr. X finished reading that article, I told him that his wife's case was similar to the one he had just read, and that he himself was responsible for it. He was rather shocked to hear such an accusation about him.

I continued, "The minds of both of you are deluded with a lot of foolish and superstitious ideas. It is absurd to believe that there are spirits, and that they can be summoned to answer questions with the help of a tumbler or a planchette.

"Jerene's mind got deranged as a result of the tumbler-talk. Being an extremely sensitive type of person whose mind, like that of yours, was indoctrinated and conditioned from childhood in superstitious beliefs about ghosts, demons, charms, poojas, hoonyams, exorcism etc., she became a victim of her own delusions.

"Though both of you placed your fingers on the tumbler, it was the psycho-motor movement of the muscles of Jerene's hand that made it move. That was why it moved again when she conducted the tumbler-talk alone at night.

"The appearance of the spirits of Mr. Bandaranaike, Madam Boonwaat and others, and the answers they are supposed to have given, are not real. Jerene herself was alarmed at the movement of the tumbler and the answers obtained. All these came from her unconscious mind without her conscious knowledge. The effects of all these strange happenings disturbed her feeble mind. Her delusional fears about the evil powers of the so-called spirits and demons which are supposed to have appeared during the tumbler-talk brought about the nervous breakdown in her.

"All her erotic experience with an imaginary St. Jude were the wish-fulfilment of a sex-starved healthy young lady whose sex glands were at their peak efficiency. From the day of the tumbler-talk she was in a neurotic state, and all her hallucinatory experiences during this period were of subjective reality to her, though not objectively factual. The visits of the romantic St. Jude, his love-making, her pregnancy, the appearance of money under her pillow, promise of the ring, promise of marriage in the next birth etc., were entirely the wishful hallucinations of her. Similarly the disappearance of her wedding ring and the ear studs, the bite and scratch marks on her body etc., were her own acts done as a dissociated personality.

"It is pity that an educated person like you, instead of consulting a psychiatrist, sought the help of charlatans who plunder money from gullible men. Probably you were encouraged to do so by the example of some of your VIP friends who consult these charlatans even for deciding matters connected with the State.

## THE REMEDY

"Jerene's troubles are purely mental, and not due to any non-existing spirits or poison or hoonyams. I can stop all these troubles today provided you are prepared to co-operate. You have to put a stop to your meditation from today, and try to play the normal role of a husband. It is foolish to abstain from a biological need, especially when your wife is in her prime of life. Had you selected an elderly person as your second wife, this sort of trouble would not have occurred.

"If you want to avoid the birth of any more children, it is wiser to seek the help of the Family Planning Clinic than meditation. It was selfish on your part to have selected a young wife, and then to go on meditating.

"Had it not been for Jerene's modest and moral upbringing, she would have satisfied her biological urge by clandestine methods. Instead, she was obtaining sex satisfaction she badly needed, through her hallucinations.

The fictitious St. Jude was only the Prince Charming of her unconscious mind."

Mr. X promised to carry out my instructions. He was then asked to go downstairs, and send his wife up. My wife made her lie down and relax on the couch. Under deep hypnosis I told her:—

"St. Jude is now before you. This is his last visit to you, and he has come to say good bye."

When I saw Jerene's facial expressions at this hypnotic suggestion, I was feeling sorry that I did not have with me then a movie camera to record on celluloid her emotional reactions at the visit of her Prince Charming.

She was further told, "St. Jude is taking away with him his child from your womb. He will never come to you again. Instead, your husband will be coming to you regularly. He will be fond of you, and you will be fond of him. Both of you will live happily with your children".

A few minutes later Mr. X left with his smiling happy wife.

A month later Mr. and Mrs. X paid us a visit with some presents to express their thanks. During our conversation I told them about the usefulness of publishing this story in countries like France, Spain and Italy, and asked their permission to do so.

"Why in those countries?", asked Jerene.

"Because, had you been in one of those countries, you would have become a Saint who got conceived by a Holy Ghost". said I.

* * *

## Chapter 18

## *SON AND MOTHER*

FIFTEEN-year-old Prema passed the G.C.f. Examination with four distinctions and three credits. Being an exceptionally bright student, the principal of her school was keen that she should enter the university, and thus bring credit to his school.

Justin Perera, a prosperous Ayurvedic physician of Negombo, was a proud father when he got a letter from Prema's principal recommending further studies for his daughter. Widower Perera had only two children—Prema and her younger brother Premakumar. Both of them attended the same mixed school.

Prema was a modest girl liked very much by her teachers and fellow students.

### TUITION

Siri Salgado, her new class teacher found that Prema needed extra help in Mathematics, and volunteered to give free tuition on Wednesdays and Fridays. As days went by her knowledge of Mathematics, and her interest in her young and handsome teacher began to improve.

Frequent appearance of new books autographed by Salgado in Prema's school-bag led to gossip among the boys and girls. These talks finally reached the ears of the principal resulting in the termination of the private tuition.

The tormented mind of Salgado urged him to pay a visit to Prema's father to stress the need for extra help for his daughter in certain subjects. The tuition which was stopped at the school at the principal's orders, was now resumed at home with the permission of the father.

### PROPOSAL

One working day when Prema was at school, Salgado paid a visit to Justin Perera and expressed his desire to marry Prema if the father was willing. As Prema was Earmarked' for Jayatissa, the son of her maternal uncle, Justin Perera declined the proposal politely. The negative reply brought tears in the eyes of the young teacher.

Moved by this pathetic sight, Perera said that he would rethink about the matter, and requested Salgado to stop the tuition.

That evening Perera asked his daughter what she thought about her teacher. "Salgado master is the best teacher in our school. All of us like him. He explains the lessons very well, and never scolds us", was the crisp reply of Prema. Perera made further enquiries about Salgado from other sources also and found that he came from a very respectable Kandyan family. He decided that Salgado was a more desirable son-in-law than his nephew Jayatissa.

Three days later Salgado received a letter from Justin Perera accepting the proposal. The formal engagement took place at a small party to which all the teachers and prefects of Prema's school were invited.

## MARRIAGE

Perera decided to conduct the wedding of his only daughter on a grand scale. With much pomp and festivity Prema's wedding took place on 18th March, 1955. Being an ayurvedic physician of repute and political influence, many politicians attended it. A Cabinet Minister and a senior Senator were the attesting witnesses.

Salgado rented out a new -small bungalow near his school, and the new couple started their married life with hope and enthusiasm without any interference from relatives. Prema stopped her studies, and devoted all her time to beautify her home. Though there was no pipe-borne water supply in the area, water was brought to the kitchen and bathroom by installing an electric pump. The kitchen was modernised with many labour-saving gadjets. With pleasure Salgado gave Prema whatever she desired except the one thing all women craved for—a child.

## SOOTHSAYERS

Justin Perera was eagerly looking for the arrival of the first grandchild in the family. Months passed into years, yet there was no visible change in Prema's vital statistics. After three years of married life, in 1958, Perera consulted an astrologer and found that according to the planetary positions Prema should have her first baby—a girl—in July 1959.

As the predicted child did not arrive even after 1960, Perera consulted a woman soothsayer of Embuldeniya. This woman looked into Anjana Eliya and said that a close relative of Perera has got a powerful charm buried in his garden with the aim of making the family extinct, and thus inherit all the wealth.

With the help of two assistants, the soothsayer woman dug out the Charm—a highly tarnished copper cylinder—from Perera's gardcn after a special pooja, and received a fee of Rs. 350. She opened the copper container in the presence of the spectators, and pulled out a tuft of human hair, a copper coin and some pieces of bones. After the charm was removed the woman said that the evil spell was over, and that Prema would get her first child—a son within twelve months.

One more year passed, yet there was no addition to the family. In 1961 Prema's mother's sister paid her a visit. During their conversation the aunt advised Prema to consult a gynaecologist. To this Prema replied, "There is no need for me to consult a doctor. Doctors cannot make a woman get a child without the co-operation of the husband". This startling reply of Prema prompted the aunt to ask her a series of questions regarding their marital life. It transpired that although the couple had married six years ago, there was no consummation of it till that day.

## LOVE POTION

This alarming news that Salgado and Prema have not yet consummated their marriage finally reached the ears of Justin Perera. The perplexed father sought the advice of his intimate friends. One of them suggested getting the aid of a reputed monk of Pasyala who used to manufacture powerful love potions. Perera went all the way to Pasyala and got a few drops of a charmed oil from the monk for Rs. 50. Perera was instructed to pour the oil into a 'suraya' (a metalic cylinder) and tie it on the girl's neck. Perera was warned by the monk that since the charm of the oil was very powerful to stimulate any male sexually, it would be necessary for the wearer to avoid going near any male other than her own husband.

Prema wore the love-potion—containing talisman from the day Perera gave it to her. Yet there was no change in Salgado's attitude towards her. Prema's aunt came once more at Perera's request to ascertain the effect of the potion. Prema told her aunt that although she had lived with her husband for seven years she was still a virgin.

## HISTORY

It was at this stage that Justin Perera was advised by a friend of his to consult me. In February 1962, just after my return from a year's stay in Europe, Perera met me at my residence. After listening to the whole story I expressed my wish to interview Prema.

Immediately after Perera left me, I wrote a letter to Siri Salgado requesting him to meet me to discuss an urgent matter. Accordingly, Salgado met me on 27th February 1962. Among other things, I gathered the following information about Salgado's past: —

Siri Salgado was the only son of Mr. and Mrs. Henry Salgado of Kandy. Henry Salgado was a prosperous lawyer of Kegalle. In 1932 two years after the birth of the son Siri Salgado, the father died of enteric.

Having lost her loving husband the widowed mother concentrated all her affection and attention on the son Siri. Even from childhood Siri was kept away from servants and other children of the neighbourhood. From the Kindergarten class upto the sixth standard the mother used to accompany Siri to his school, and stay there till evening. Even when he was a big boy the mother used to feed him herself. Till Siri joined the Peradeniya University, he slept on the same bed with the mother. While he was at the university hostel Siri used to spend sleepless nights being home-sick. When he came home during vacation he continued his old habit of sleeping on the same bed with the-mother. His mother too was extremely unhappy if her 'child'—now a grown up youth—was not in bed with her. Siri and his mother could not exist without each other.

After graduating, Siri did not like the idea of seeking any job which would necessitate his leaving the mother. He, therefore, accepted a teacher's job in Kegalle itself. His whole salary was brought home every month and given to the mother.

In 1953 Mrs. Salgado died of heart failure. From the day he lost his mother Siri lost all interest in life. Several times he thought of committing suicide.

The principal of Siri's school, a very sympathetic type of man, helped Siri to get a transfer to a school at Negombo.

On the first day of his arrival at the new school the principal took Siri to the newly formed University Entrance class, of which he was meant to be the class-teacher.

Siri was a happy man once again. Without his conscious knowledge he developed a mental elation. Everything at Negombo and at his new school turned out to be very pleasant. Though he was an introvert all his life, he started talking to all and sundry.

What was the secret of this sudden change in Siri? On the first day when the principal took him to his new class, Siri found a face similar to that of his dead mother. That was the face of Prema. The unconscious satisfaction of seeing his mother daily in the person of Prema made Siri like the new school and all the people he met at Negombo.

It was not with any romantic motive that Siri volunteered to give free tuition to Prema, but the awakened interest in his neurotic mind. He wanted to marry her not because he wanted her as a sex partner, but because of his unconscious desire to live and sleep with his mother-substitute. He did not even touch her body. Salgado loved Prema with all his heart. It was not the carnal love of a romantic lover, but the love of a devoted son towards his devoted mother.

## AMMA

A couple of days later Justin Perera came with his daughter while Siri Salgado was at school. From Prema I was able to gather a lot more information about the married life of the couple.

Prema loved her husband deeply as he was very compassionate, trustworthy and deeply affectionate to her. Siri never did anything without consulting her or against her wish. His entire salary was entrusted to her. It was she who gave him money even for his personal use.

Though they slept side by side, she never exposed her body in his presence, nor did he in her presence. Siri called Prema endearingly as Amma.

Though she craved for a child, and he did nothing to fulfil her desire, Prema was not prepared to divorce him, and marry someone else who would be a real husband to her. In her sleep she used to dream of having sex with him, and experience orgasm.

## REMEDY

In my counsel to Prema I told her, "Sex is only a biological function of the body like any other physiological functions. Since it is connected with the propagation of the species, it is not only a personal need but also a social need. Just as hunger is satisfied by consuming food, and thirst by drinking water, sex is satisfied by mating with a person of the opposite sex. Unlike other biological functions, man has made certain rules and regulations in mating for the sake of harmonious life in society. These rules are necessary because, unlike other bodily functions such as nutrition, respiration, blood-circulation, excretion etc., in mating another individual also is involved. Such marital rules and customs vary from place to place, society to society, religion to religion and time to time. There is nothing sacred about these rules and regulations connected with sex.

"Animals, not being so intelligent as men to make rules and laws, are not inhibited by moral codes. In the society we are living at present it is legitimate to satisfy sex by mating with a person of the opposite sex who has entered into a contract to do so by marriage. In seeking satisfaction both husband and wife have equal rights.

"Your husband's sex attraction towards you is very badly distorted because he is a victim of a mental disease. This originated in him from childhood by the folly of his ignorant mother. Had he been brought up like normal children he would have proved to be a very good husband for you. Unless this mental complex is radically removed from him he will continue to love you only as his mother, and not as his wife. I know of another victim of this malady who too was the only child of a rich widow. Even after his marriage to a pretty wife, the young man continued to sleep with his mother leaving his young bride to sleep in another room. This unfortunate wife is now an inmate of a mental hospital.

"The remedy for making your married life a success is entirely with you. If you can follow my advice from today you are sure to succeed in removing the wrong attitude from your husband.

"You have waited all these years for your husband to make advances towards you. Now it is your turn to take the initiative. It is perfectly legitimate and modest for a wife to do so to her husband. It is your right as a wife.

"Erotic feelings in a person can be roused through the five senses. If you take the initiative you will be able to stimulate sex desire in your partner by suitable behaviour patterns. Even less intelligent animals adopt such techniques. Although mothers do not expose their bodies before their grown-up sons, it is perfectly normal and desirable for a wife to do so before her husband in privacy. Unlike a mother, a wife need not be fully clad when she goes to bed with her husband. A wife has every right to discuss sexual matters with her husband. She has also every right to touch or caress any part of her husband's body. It is left for you to throw away your false modesty in the privacy of your bed-room and stimulate your husband erotically. Such actions from you will make his conscious mind realise that you are no more his mother, but his wife. It is sure to remove the neurotic complex from your husband's unconscious mind."

Prema left me after receiving certain post-hypnotic suggestions given under deep hypnosis.

In January 1964, Siri Salgado, Prema and their little son paid us a New-Year visit. When I took the chubby baby in my arms I was able to see the expression of happiness and gratitude in the tears that dripped down Prema's cheeks.

## Chapter 19

### *FIERY PHANTOM'*

TIKIRI SENA was a feudal chief living in a palatial 'Radella Walauwa' in a two hundred acre coconut estate in a place situated between the 'Uda Rata' and 'Patha Ratha' countries. In 1951 there was big trouble for Tikiri Sena and his vassals in the 'Nindagama'. This had nothing to do with the big flood of that year, nor was it due to any dispute between the lord and his vassals. Tikiri Sena was one of those few feudal chiefs who were considerate and kind to his vassals. He had allowed about fifty families of villagers to continue to stay in the extensive lands he inherited from his ancestors. They were staying in this estate and taking the produce from it from the time of Tikiri Sena's father. Mrs. Tikiri Sena too was very kind to these villagers.

By nature Tikiri Sena was a timid type of person without any particular ambition in life. Though he led a comfortable lazy life, he and his wife took a keen interest in the welfare of the villagers in the hamlet on the estate. This Tikiri Sena did without any political or selfish motive, for politics was beyond his capacity. His main hobby was to read the daily newspapers from the first page to the last giving special care to the column 'What the stars Foretell'.

Jamis and Peter and their wives were the domestic aid at the Walauwa. They came daily to the palatial bungalow at about 5 a.m. In the evening while the two women went back home before dusk, their husbands Jamis and Peter departed for home only after 10 p.m. after their master and his family had gone to bed.

### HUE AND CRY

One day at about 11 p.m. soon after Tikiri Sena and family had gone to bed they heard a hue and cry from the direction of the hamlet. Instead of getting up and enquiring about what was happening, Tikiri Sena switched off the lights and closed and bolted all the windows and doors of his bed-room. He called his eldest son, 20 years old, who had come home for the holidays from his school in Kandy that morning, and was sleeping in his room downstairs, and asked him to close all the windows and doors of his room. That night Tikiri Sena could not get a wink of sleep. He thought murder or some such thing had taken place in the hamlet.

Peter and his wife failed to come to the Walauwa next morning at the usual time 5 a.m. whereas Jamis and his wife came as usual. Peter and his wife arrived after daybreak. The four servants, instead of starting their routine work, were talking among themselves about a mysterious flame of fire which all of them saw the previous night. This fire was seen moving to and fro along the lane leading to the hamlet. When Tikiri Sena and family came out of their rooms in the morning Peter and the other three servants told them with excitement and fear all what they had seen the previous night. They said, "At about 11 p.m. last night we saw a huge flame floating about six feet in the air moving up and down the lane several times and finally disappear."

## FEAR

The whole of that day this was the topic of conversation among the residents of the hamlet. Next night too the fire appeared in the lane exactly at 11 p.m. More people, including the members of Tikiri Sena's family, saw the flame this time. By the third day the news about the floating fire in the lane spread into the neighbouring villages and large crowds began to collect at the Walauwa.

From that day almost all the people in the neighbourhood were struck by a sort of intense fear. Children in all the houses were put to sleep by 7 p.m. Nobody ventured out of the house after sunset. Workers in the fields returned home before dusk. Jamis, Peter and the two women left the Walauwa for home before nightfall. They came back to bungalow in the morning only after daybreak.

## OPINIONS

Villagers started giving their own interpretations about this mysterious phenomenon. Some said it was a Gini-pillaya'—a flaming ghost—roaming about for a victim. Others said it was the ghost of Bandara, who was murdered in the lane some two years ago. Some others said it was a 'Devatha Eliya'—light of gods. A few others said it was the gem of 'Bhairavaya'.

The regular appearance of this mobile fire at night meant immense trouble for Tikiri Sena and family. Though blessed with immense wealth they could not exist even for a single day without their servant's help. Tikiri Sena was incapable of even taking his own daily bath without the assistance of Jamis. The part played by Tikiri Sena during his own bath was to simply sit on a stool in the bath-room. It was the work of Jamis to apply soap and scrub his master's body, pour a hundred and one buckets of water on the head, and finally wipe the body dry. The insistance of all the servants to leave for home before nightfall meant complete incapacitation for Tiki Sena's household after 6 p.m.

Villagers who used to assemble at the Walauwa during the day were not slow to give liberally helpful suggestions to get rid of this troubling ghost. Names of numerous powerful 'kattadiyas' near and far were mentioned. It was at this stage that a young man who had come from Colombo to meet Tikiri Sena's eldest son, suggested to consult me. At a small conference of all the members of Tikiri Sena's family and the new visitor from Colombo, it was decided to seek my assistance.

## RESCUE

Tikiri Sena met me at my residence on the morning of a Saturday in April 1951. A vivid description of all what had happened was given to me. After listening patiently I agreed to go over to the Walauwa next day, but Tikiri Sena insisted that I must accompany him the same day.

Myself and Tikiri Sena left my house at about 10 a.m. There was a short stay in the Fort for about 20 minutes to enable Tikiri Sena to make some purchases. The driver brought a large parcel and deposited in the luggage boot of Tikiri Sena's car. We drove in heavy rain a long way through winding and sometimes partially submerged roads to reach Tikiri Sena's bungalow by about 3 p.m.

Soon after reaching the Walauwa both Tikiri Sena and myself took a wash, and had tea served in the garden. As the servants were anxious to go home early, dinner was served at about 6 p.m. While looking at the rich menu my mind flashed back to the time I had to wait alone in the car in the Fort. The 20 minutes' waiting was not in vain!

The servants did not wait to finish the washing up. They dumped everything into the pantry and dashed off home with "chulu" lights in their hands.

As the sky cleared up and the quarter moon could be seen through the palm fronds, we decided to go sit out in the garden and talk. During this talk Tikiri Sena consumed a liberal quantity of "Johnny Walker" with myself keeping company with lesser quantities at longer intervals.

## GHOST APPEARS

At about 11 p.m. they heard a few 'hoos' from the hamlet. Mrs. Tikiri Sena stood up and screamed, "There, there, there is the Ginipilliya". All of them stood up motionless and looked in the direction of the distant lane.

The fire could be seen clearly floating in the air and moving to the east. It moved to a distance of about 100 yards, and then started moving to the west. The flame was about one foot broad and two feet high. I stood up and watched. I then called Tikiri Sena and his son to come with me towards the fire. Both of them refused and wanted to go inside the house. I then asked for a walking stick, and armed with the walking stick I walked briskly towards the lane. As I neared the lane I could see the flame very distinctly.

It appeared to be suspended in the air about six feet from the ground, and as I entered the lane the flame was receding from me. I walked faster and faster to reach the fire. It was now about fifty yards in front of me.

CHASE

Then it became stationary for a moment and started coming towards me. I stopped walking and stood motionless. As the flame came nearer and nearer, I could see below the fire a hazy human-like figure hands outstretched and with legs that seemed to dangle below. As the flame came nearly 10 yards from me, I shouted at the top of my voice, "Stop there, who are you". To my surprise the flame dropped on the ground and the dangling human-like figure started running away. I gave chase. From the lane the human-like figure ran into the coconut estate with myself at his heels.

After running for about sixty yards in the estate the figure accidentally fell into a square pit prepared for planting coconut seedlings. I pounced on it with the agility of a panther and held him down.

"Mahatayo, please don't kill me. I am Jamis who served food for you", said the ghostly figure.

He held my feet and begged me for pardon.

"Why are you doing this nonsense?" I asked.

"Mahataya, please come with me to my house and I will tell you the whole truth", said Jamis.

Both Jamis and myself, panting for breath, walked back to the place where the flame was thrown down. Jamis picked up a large saucepan from the ground, and requested me to go with him to his hut nearby. As we got in Jamis asked me to sit on the dilapidated bed in his one roomed hut, and started narrating his story with tears in his eyes.

"I was born and brought up in this estate", Jamis said, "My father and mother worked for Walauwa Hamuduruwo's father. I too started working for Walauwa Hamuduruwo from my childhood. Hamuduruwo is my everything and I am his. I got married some six months ago. My wife too works at the Walauwa. My wife comes home in the evening earlier than I, to attend to some of our own household work. I can leave the Walauwa only by 10 p.m.

"During the last school holidays when Podi Hamaduruwo came home from Kandy, he used to come to my hut after nightfall and trouble my young and attractive wife. Even our lives will be in danger if this affair is made known to any one. From the day Podi Hamuduruwo came home this time I started walking along the lane a few times with burning coconut shells in this saucepan filled with paddy husks. Since I started this, we have no trouble from Podi Hamuduruwo. Mahatayo, I will not do this again. Please don't tell this to Walauwa Hamuduruwo or any one else," Jamis repeatedly begged me not to divulge the secret.

## TRIUMPH

I went back to the Walauwa triumphantly. I saw Tikiri Sena, his wife and the son (Podi Hamuduruwo) standing on the verandah anxiously waiting for me. "I caught the Ginipilliya", I shouted, "Ginipilliya has promised me that it will not come to the estate any more." I slept that night at the Walauwa and returned to Colombo the next morning.

A week later a huge car drove up to the porch of my house in Colombo. The driver carried into my bungalow a box and two hampers—one of flowers and the other of fruits and vegetables. The box contained bottles of whisky, tins of biscuits and balls of cheese. Mr. and Mrs. Tikiri Sena departed leaving a permanent invitation to myself and my wife to visit the Walauwa every time we go to the hills.

## Chapter 20

### *THE LIGHT READER WHO HELPED TO TRACE A MISSING GIRL*

From time immemorial necromancy in Sri Lanka, was the monopoly of Malayalees. In this trade the shrewd Malayalees found very good scope for amassing wealth. With the adoption of stringent immigration laws by the Government, a few enterprising Sinhalese have stepped into this business left behind by the numerous Malayalees who were forced to leave this country. But, to be a successful black magician in Sri Lanka one has to be a Malayalee or a disciple of a Malayalee "professor", for persons from Kerala are reputed in this country as masters of black art. Many Malayalees who have come here have helped to sustain this reputation by sheer pretension and bluff.

On 20th April 1963 there appeared in the Ceylon Daily News a news item under the headline "LIGHT READER HELPED TO TRACE GIRL WHO WAS KIDNAPPED". The first paragraph of this report was thus:—

"A light reader had helped to trace a young girl who had been kidnapped. He had given the correct number of the taxi in which the girl was taken, as well as the direction in which the taxi went. This was stated before Mr. J. Senathirajah, Acting Chief Magistrate of Colombo in a case in which W. Kumaratunga and W. Amaratunga, both of Madampitiya Road, Grandpass, were accused of kidnapping a 15-year-old girl from the lawful guardianship of her father E. P. S. Raman of Madampitiya Road, Manager of a toddy tavern."

Soon after this appeared in the papers, I received a number of letters asking what I had to say about this miraculous power of the light-reader.

## INVESTIGATION BEGINS

On April 26th 1963 I set out to this place called Madampitiya. As I was a stranger to this place I stopped my car in front of a small tea boutique to make enquiries. To my pleasant surprise I found that the owner of the boutique was a Malayalee by name Raghavan, who had married a Ceylonese by 'descent' and thus established his claim for Ceylon citizenship. Raghavan was very happy to see another Malayalee in me.

On explaining the main aim of my mission Raghavan's face brightened as he knew everything about this case. Raghavan volunteered to take me to Pappu, the reputed Malayalee black artist who was responsible for giving the correct number of the taxi in which Raman's 15-year-old daughter was kidnapped. Raghavan got into my car and both of us drove to a distance of about two miles to the residence of Pappu.

Raghavan's tea boutique is the rendezvous of the few Malayalees still remaining in this part of Colombo. There are two toddy taverns here, one of which managed by Raman, the kidnapped girl's father. Raghavan's income from the tea boutique is just enough to support his 'local' wife and two children. Due to Exchange control restrictions he does not send money now to his Malayalee wife and children at his "Rajyam". In addition to his income from the tea boutique he, being a Malayalee, is able to earn some extra income by practising a bit of "Manthras" whenever he gets suitable clients.

Pappu, the professional black magician is really a Sinhalese who has now become a Malayalee for the sake of his profession. Though not able to read and write Malayalam, Pappu is capable of speaking that language fluently. Raman, the kidnapped girl's father is a Malayalee. He lived with his Malayalee wife and three daughters about 2 furlongs away from Raghavan's boutique. After the kidnapping incident they have shifted to another place away from Kumaratunga's house. Raman and his wife were aware that their 15-year-old eldest daughter was on friendly terms with their neighbour's son W. Kumaratunga. The girl eloped with Kumaratunga on 21st January 1963 at about 9 p.m. when the parents were away at a wedding party in a neighbouring house.

## LIGHT READER

In about 15 minutes Raghavan and myself reached the residence of Pappu in Silver Smith Lane, Colombo-12. There were three other cars parked in front of the house. “Professor” Pappu’s sign board had writings in English, Sinhalese, Tamil and Malayalam. From the verandah of Pappu’s house we walked into a reception room. The two benches and a few chairs in that waiting room were fully occupied by men and women waiting for their turn to be called into the Sanctum Sanctorum. Pappu’s Sinhalese wife, dressed like a typical Malayalee village woman, acted as the receptionist giving instructions to the clients regarding the type of offerings and payments they are expected to make before Pappu. She enters into a subtle conversation with them and makes a study of their problems. On and off she goes into the Sanctorum on the pretext of feeding the wicks in the brass oil lamp near Pappu’s seat, and has a word or two with him in whisper.

Raghavan appeared to be a privileged person in this place for without waiting in the queue he asked me to remove my shoes and follow him into the inner chamber. We walked into a 10 feet square, ill-ventilated room filled with fumes from burning camphor and coconut oil. In the centre of the floor was a triangular pit with fire for burning camphor. All around this pit was placed various kinds of offerings such as husked coconuts planted vertically on heaps or rice, paddy, gingily seeds, puffed rice etc. There were also fruits of various kinds in plenty. Money, folded in betel leaves, is solemnly placed in the hands of Pappu, who is seated cross-legged in the remote dark corner of this room just behind a decorated box which resembled a small pigeon-house. Pappu looked like a typical ‘Sanyasi’ with long hair and beard, and the body profusely branded with ‘holy ash’. All the available space on the walls was filled with framed pictures of diverse types of polycephalic and multilimbed gods garlanded with faded jasmine flowers. Also there were brass and earthen images of gods and demons placed at the four corners. With all these conglomerates. the place looked like a shrine room.

At the time Raghavan and myself entered the room Pappu was engaged in consultation with a client. While answering this client's questions Pappu was seen looking into the box in front through a pigeon-hole door. Raghavan and myself took our seats on the floor close to the box. Attracted by the special treatment I was receiving, 10 or 12 inquisitive persons also flocked into the room and stood behind me. Just when the client got up Raghavan introduced me to Pappu as an investigator and writer. Pappu appeared to like the idea of getting publicity.

Without wasting any time Pappu started a small sermon giving an account of his past achievements, and how he acquired mastery in his wonderful art at the feet of genuine Malayalee 'gurus'. His real name is Harumanis Berera. "Pappu" is the name given him by his four Malayalee 'gurus' Krishna Panikkar, Kumara Panikkar, Damodara Panikkar and Govinda Panikkar all brothers from Kunnamkulam in Kerala State. All of them left the shores of Lanka when the Japanese dropped a few bombs in Colombo. Pappu claimed to have solved many crimes by his occult powers. He gets correct answers by looking into 'Anjanameliya'. When Raman and his wife came to him in January to consult about their kidnapped daughter, he gave them the correct number of the taxi in which she was removed.

## THE TEST

In the presence of the small crowd in the room I took out a five rupee currency note from my wallet and kept it folded in my left palm, and requested Pappu to look into the 'anjanameliya' and give the serial number on the currency note. After about 2 minutes' continuous looking into the box Pappu started dictating the number with ample pause after each digit. I gave a paper and pencil to Raghavan for jotting down the number. As a counter check I myself took down the number in my book. The number given by Pappu was S|45-90283. I opened the note in my hand and showed it to Pappu, Raghavan and all others who were in the room. The number of the note was G|51-398415. Nobody uttered a word in the room.

Although Pappu failed to give the correct number, I was simply admiring his power of observation in reproducing the pattern of numbering on such currency notes, viz., a vulgar fraction followed by a six-digit number. But this admiration lasted only till I peeped into the pigeonhole of Pappu's box. In this box, with a pile of other currency notes I saw a five rupee note open on the top. I put my five rupees back into my wallet, thanked Pappu and the rest of the people there and departed. As I was getting into the car, Raghavan whispered into my ear, "Noon time is extremely unsuited for looking into "Anjanameliya".

The next day I interviewed the police officer who investigated the case in his office at the Grand pass Police Station. The facts obtained from him are thus:—The kidnapping incident was reported to the police station on 21st January 1963 at 10.30 p.m. The name of suspect was given. Immediately radio messages were given to all the Police Stations in the Island to be on the look out for a runaway couple. On suspicion, the police on beat duty at Ambalangoda arrested a taxi in which a girl and two young boys were seen proceeding in the direction of Galle. They were brought to the Grandpass Police Station the next morning. Nobody gave the number of the taxi to the police.

The same evening I met Raman, the father of the kidnapped girl, at his new residence at Kotahena. To the question what made him tell the prosecuting lawyer about the light-reader giving the correct number of the taxi, Raman's reply was short and crisp. "That sir, is the best way to make the local fellows understand that it is dangerous to 'play' with a Malayalee."

# Chapter 21

## *THE POLTERGEIST*

The inmates of Mr. Eliezer's house other than himself were Mrs. Eliezer, his mother (Mrs. Eliezer Sr.), his four children, a middle-aged servant woman and a 13-year-old servant girl. After a thorough inspection of the entire house and its surroundings, myself and my wife took our seats by the side of the dining table. We interrogated all the members of the household individually, one after the other except the youngest two children. My wife assisted me in taking down notes. I insisted that I wanted evidence, only about those things seen with their own eyes, and not what they have heard from other inmates of the house.

During this investigation it transpired that Mrs. Eliezer was away in a Nursing Home for about fifteen days to give birth to her youngest child. Stones continued to fall in the house while she was away from the home. She had come back from the Nursing Home only two days ago. During the time of questioning I carefully observed the behaviour of each and every person.

### POLTERGEIST

After all the investigations were over I asked all the inmates of the house to assemble in the drawing room. Turning to Mr. Eliezer I said, "Since you all are educated persons capable of rational thinking, I like to explain to you my findings. From the available evidence it has to be accepted that stones and money were thrown into the house. There is absolutely no evidence to conclude that stones rose up from the court-yard alone and flew into the house. Also there is no evidence to say that big stones came through small holes.

"In the absence of living bodies capable of performing metabolic functions it is not possible for the so-called bodyless spirits to generate energy to project stones and money. Also, in the absence of the brain and associated nervous tissues it is not possible for the 'spirits' to perform conscious acts. Thus we have to conclude that a human agent is behind all these incidents. It cannot be an enemy of the family because it is not natural for any one to throw money at an enemy.

"Absence of throws between 11 p.m. and 7 a.m. indicates that the person goes to sleep during that time. I have not heard of 'spirits' resting between 11 p.m. and 7 a.m. Since stones fell in the house even when all the doors and windows were closed, I conclude that it was done by an inmate of the house, who can be called by the German name 'Poltergeist'".

## GHOSTS

"This type of 'poltergeist phenomena' is not peculiar to this country alone. All over the world such things happen, and the common belief is that a poltergeist is a mysterious 'spirit'. But I tell you, it is neither mysterious nor spiritual. Such wrong beliefs are sustained due to lack of scientific investigation. If the investigators happen to be believers in the mysterious powers of the so-called 'spirits', it is quite natural for them to attribute all inexplicable incidents to such spirits. As I proceed on the basis that there are no ghosts—evil, good or 'holy' —all my attention during the investigation is directed to find out the human agent responsible for the whole affair, and so far I have never failed to detect the person concerned. The so-called occultists and exorcists, who are generally consulted at such times also help to confirm the wrong beliefs that poltergeists are spirits."

## ABNORMAL

A Poltergeist is nothing but a mentally sick person. This type of mental abnormality results generally from some sort of frustration. Often it is found in children of adolescent age, but I know of one case where the poltergeist happened to be an adult—a mother of two children.

"As they do all these mischievous acts in a schizophrenic state, under normal conditions they will not be able to recall to their conscious memory what they have done in their split personality. By hetero-suggestive methods it is possible to make them accept what they have done in the schizophrenic state. Those mischievous acts done by the split personality are so skilfully done as to prevent detection by others. Once the poltergeist is caught in the act, the trouble will invariably stop from then. In my experience I have found that such persons are of feeble mind and can be brought under hypnosis by hetero-suggestion. A promise extracted under such conditions is seldom broken.

"Here in this house the poltergeist can be any one except your wife and the youngest two children. I rule out your wife because the trouble in the house continued even when she was away at the Nursing Home. In my investigation I do not generally divulge the identity of the 'poltergeist' to the inmates of the house, in order to prevent the poor person becoming an object of hatred or curiosity, and thus aggravating the mental derangement. As I find you are an understanding type of person I am going to tell you who the poltergeist in this house is. It is the younger of the two servant girls you have. She should not be punished or reprimanded for causing you mental agony and financial loss. She was not doing all these things out of hatred towards any one of you. They are not her conscious acts. She needs kind and compassionate treatment."

## PROTEST

When I declared the thirteen-year-old girl as the poltergeist, there was vigorous protest from Mr. Eliezer's mother. She assured us that on more occasions than one stones have fallen in the house when the girl was near her. "Even this afternoon it was she who shouted out when the stones fell", said Mrs. Eliezer (Sr.)

"You yourself can establish the identity of the poltergeist by isolating each and every member of the family individually for a couple of days", I told her, "It may be you or Mr. Eliezer himself, but I am positive that it is this girl".

At this stage Mr. Eliezer said that he would send the girl next day to his brother's house and keep her there for a few days and see the effect.

At about 9 p.m. we got into our car to depart. When I was about to start the car my wife told me, "I don't think they are convinced. They may not even take the trouble of testing by isolating the girl." I pondered for a moment, got out of the car, and requested Mr. Eliezer to put two chairs out in the court-yard. We took our seats in the semi-dark court-yard, and asked Mr. Eliezer to send the young girl to us.

I drew a circle with my finger on the ground and asked the girl to stand motionless in it. After a few minutes of hetero-suggestive talk by me the girl got into a semi-hypnotic state and started narrating all what she did, She accepted that she was responsible for all the incidents which took place in the house. She explained how she got money for throwing by saving small amounts from the cash given her for marketing. She also told how, she used to collect stones from near the fence during the day and store them in a tin kept hidden under the fire-wood in the kitchen.

One day when all the grown up members of the house had gone to the Nursing Home to see the new-born baby, she gave a hard blow to the leg of the Alsation dog with the wooden handle of the broom. It was from that day that the dog started limping.

I made the girl promise that she would never in future do such mischievous acts. In return I promised her that she would not be subjected to any type of punishment for her actions in the past.

We went back to the house and spoke to Mr. Eliezer and other members of the family who were anxiously waiting to know the result:—

"As I suspected all of you were a bit sceptical over my analysis, I decided, much against my wish and usual practice, to make the girl own up. Now she has confessed everything to me, but I request you neither to question her nor to treat her as a suspect. If she is not treated kindly, there is every chance of her becoming a subject of chronic hysteria."

The faces of all, including that of the doubting mother brightened up with an expression of relief. The eldest of the children was heard to say, "Now there is nothing to prevent us from celebrating Christmas happily." We left triumphantly at 10 p.m.

The girl continued to serve Eliezers for about two years more without creating any trouble whatsoever.

## *Chapter 22*

## *THE GHOST OF THE LIVING*

It happened during the last world war. Leelawathy of Akmimana in the Galle District, a simple and innocent village girl, was looked upon by other young women of the neighbourhood with envy. Unlike them, she always had money in her purse.

The village hawker Meera Lebbe made it a point to visit Leelawathy every Wednesday. He found in Leelawathy a very good customer for the knick-knacks he peddled along with assorted textiles. Lebbe's weekly visits to Leelavathy attracted all the young women and girls in the neighbourhood to her house. They simply came to feast their eyes on the various attractive merchandise in Lebbe's mobile show-case on wheels pulled and sometimes pushed by young Sarath. Though these articles were beyond their means, they all derived pleasure in selecting good articles for Leelawathy to buy.

Appuhamy, Leelawathy's father, was a salesman at a grocery shop at Galle bazaar. Daily he left home early in the morning and came back at about 9 p.m. Leelawathy aged 24 and her step-sister Siriyawathy aged 10, dutifully attended to the household chores. After the death of Leelawathy's mother, Appuhamy took a second wife. But she too died a few months after giving birth to Siriyawathy. It was left to the lot of Leelawathy to bring up her motherless step-sister.

### MARRIAGE

Somapala, son of a farmer in the same village, after failing the J.S.C. Examination was employed as a junior clerk in the same shop where Appuhamy worked. Along with some of his old classmates, Somapala had applied for enlistment in the army. It was at this time that Appuhamy got Somapala to marry Leelawathy. After the marriage Somapala lived with Leelawathy in Appuhamy's house.

Exactly forty days after the wedding, Somapala was called up to report at the Army Headquarters in Colombo. Leelawathy had to bid farewell to her young husband in tears. Next evening Appuhamy, Leelawathy and Siriyawathy saw Somapala off at the Galle Railway Station. After four months of intensive training at Diyatalawa Camp, Somapala was sent with a contingent of fifty other Ceylonese lads to a theatre of war.

## LONG SEPARATION

The mental worry in Leelawathy caused by the separation from her loving husband was amply compensated by Somapala's regular letters and her share in his monthly salary, which reached her every month by post. She took pride in showing Somapala's photos in corporal's uniform to all and sundry. She must have shown the same pictures about four or five times to Lebbe and his assistant Sarath.

Unlike other girls in the village Leelawathy did not waste her time in gossip. After sending Siriyawathy to school, and finishing the household chores, she engaged herself in weaving pillow-lace. By selling these laces to Lebbe during his weekly visits she made additional pocket money. Except for the routine visits of Lebbe and Sarath there were no other male visitors to this house when Appuhamy was away.

Although she could read Somapala's letters with great difficulty, Leelawathy was incapable of writing replies to Somapala. On two occasions she sought the help of Sarath to write replies to Somapala. It could be said that the correspondence between Somapala and his wife was virtually a one-way-traffic. But this too did not last long. Letters from Somapala gradually became few and far between, and finally it terminated completely. But the monthly Money Order continued to arrive without any break.

## GLOOM

Leelawathy's happy days seem to have left her by now.

Absence of letters from Somapala began to give her a lot of mental worry. Lebbe began to discover that his weekly visits to her was getting less and less profitable. Instead of buying articles from them, Leelawathy was making use of their visits to give vent to her mental worry. She made Sarath write a letter on her behalf imploring Somapala to write her at least one more letter. Yet there was no response.

Having lost a good market in Leelawathy's house Meera Lebbe ceased his weekly visits. The end of Lebbe's business-visits was the beginning of Sarath's social-visits. Sarath worked for Lebbe on a daily wage from 8 a.m. to 5 p.m.

Out of pity for Leelawathy Sarath occasionally came to her house in the evening and spent some time 'consoling' her. Sarath told her how even the best-behaved boys get spoiled after joining the army; how soldiers spend their money on wayward women and how some of them even marry foreign girls. Leelawathy listened to all these stories with tears in her eyes. She told him how much better it would have been for Somapala to have continued to work as a clerk in the shop at Galle even though the salary was small.

DANGER

Sarath's visits to Leelavathy became more frequent. It now became a routine act with Sarath to take a bath in the evening after the day's rounds with Lebbe, change into good dress, and make a bee-line to Leelawathy. He generally left Leelawathy's house by about 8 p.m. The frequent visits of Sarath had a balmy effect on Leelawathy's sorrow-stricken mind As days went by the thoughts about Somapala began to diminish in her mind in direct proportion to the frequency of Sarath's visits and the growth of the abdominal girth. But Sarath's visit to Leelawathy became lesser and lesser as the result of their friendship was getting more and more conspicuous in her. Finally he disappeared completely from Akmimana.

Since Appuhamy left for work daily very early in the morning and returned late at night, he did not know for a long time what was happening at home in his absence. Moreover since Leelawathy led an unblemished life in her 'teens, Appuhamy least thought of giving her special protection after her marriage. Later, when he came to know the real state of affairs he decided to be reconciled with the situation, and allowed things to take their own course.

## 'UNWANTED'

In August 1946 Leelawathy gave birth to a boy. Appuhamy consulted the local astrologer and got the child's horoscope written. According to it the child was destined to acquire great learning and wealth, go across the seas, become a leader of men, have a lot of influential friends and marry a rich girl. His bad time would be the first five years under the influence of Saturn.

Leelawathy brought up the child with all the instinctive maternal affection in her. Appuhamy found in this child a prosperous evening for his life. He advised Leelawathy to take special care to protect the child during the first five Saturn years.

## 'POSSESSED'

On Monday 11th November 1946 Leelavathy got a telegram from Army Headquarters intimating her of the death of Somapala in action. Her cry attracted people from the neighbourhood. They tried to console her in vain. A messenger was sent to Appuhamy. When Appuhamy came home at 12 p.m. he saw there a sympathetic and helpful crowd. Another messenger was sent to convey the sad news to Somapala's parents.

As Leelawathy showed signs of complete collapse, Appuhamy did not go to work next day. At about 4 p.m. that day, when there were still a few close relatives at home, Leelawathy stood up with outstretched hands. Her body became stiff and the eyes started rolling. Gradually her whole body began to exhibit spasmodic twitches. She started shouting in a manly voice, "I will teach you a lesson. You have cheated my wife. I will kill you and your child. I have seen human blood. I have shot many men. I will go only after killing Sarath and his child." Leelawathy fell to the ground after the trance and lay motionless for about fifteen minutes.

All who assembled there confirmed that it was Somapala's spirit which got into Leelawathy. Not only did she speak like him but her voice and language simulated that of Somapala. Friends of the family were concerned about the safety of Leelawathy's child, because when she got 'possessed' she attempted to kill him. Appuhamy decided to send the child to his sister's house, but Leelawathy refused. She was extremely fond of her child. It was only when Somapala's spirit got into her that she disliked the child and wanted to kill him.

From that day onwards Leelawathy got 'possessed' every day after dinner. In the 'possessed' state she used to march militarily round the house shouting—left-right-left-right. . . . Sometimes she shouted murderous threats against Sarath who was not anywhere there.

During the day when Appuhamy was away from home Leelawathy remained quite normal, hence her child could safely be left with her at that time. At night the child slept with Appuhamy.

THOVIL'

After some days Appuhamy decided to drive Somapala's ghost from the house by conducting a 'thovil' ceremony. Capable 'kattadiyas' were brought from Gintota, and the ceremony was conducted on a grand scale. During the ceremony, at about midnight, in the midst of frenzied drumming and dancing by six 'kattadiyas' Leelawathy got 'possessed' and started dancing about with the kattadiyas. The drumming and the dancing came to an abrupt stop. The chief kattadiya touched Leelawathy's forehead with a magic wand and asked her a series of questions. Leelawathy gave the following answers in broken sentences:—

"I am Somapala. I came in a ship to Galle. I came to see my wife. Sarath has cheated my wife. I do not want my wife to keep his child. I want to kill Sarath and the child. I will go away only if you sacrifice two lives. I am prepared to go on to the old jak tree in the garden. I will shake a branch of the tree as a sign that I have gone."

After this ecstatic dance and talk Leelawathy fell down in a faint. The roosters were sacrificed as wanted by Somapala's spirit. While Leelawathy was still lying on the floor, the chief 'kattadiya' went to the jak tree to make sure that Somapala's ghost has entered it. The crowd too followed him. He looked up the tree and shouted to the ghost to shake one branch as a sign. He was satisfied that one branch shook though nobody else saw it. The time was 1 a.m. The chief 'kattadiya's authoritative opinion was that the restless ghost of Somapala came all the way to Akmimana to join his wife because he was not given a proper burial with religious rites.

For two weeks after the 'thovil' Leelawathy was quite normal. But after partaking a curry made with a jak fruit from the same tree now haunted by Somapala's spirit, Leelawathy started getting possessed again.

## GLASSOLALIA

At this time I was at Richmond College, Galle. Piyadasa, Appuhamy's employer and a friend of mine came with Appuhamy to my residence in Chando Street in the Galle Fort, to seek my help. Appuhamy gave a detailed description of everything that had happened, and I made copious notes. After listening to the whole story I told Piyadasa, "There is no need for me to come with you. It is not Somapala's ghost that is troubling Leelawathy. Instead, of saying that she is possessed of his spirit, it is more correct to say that she is merely imitating Somapala. It is simply the effect of her own hallucinations brought about by her guilty conscience and foolish beliefs. There is absolutely no scientific evidence to say that ghosts of dead persons exist, and that living persons can get 'possessed' of them. Some persons, as the result of a schizoid mental state known as glassolalia behave like 'possessed' persons simulating the language, speech, voice and even the actions of dead or believed-to-be-dead persons. Such paranormal aberrations in feeble-minded persons are often mistakenly attributed to 'possession' of evil or holy spirits, rebirths, revelations or as effects of charms and curses.

"I have witnessed such bizarre behaviour due to attacks of glassolalia more among persons with parathyroid deficiency at 'thovil' and 'bali' ceremonies and at some religious 'revivals' where the devotee claim to get divine power to speak in "tongues". Due to the ignorance about this type of schizoid phenomenon many exorcists, like the 'kattadiyas' and some priests still believe the existence of ghosts-and 'possessions'. The chief kattadiya from Gintota mast have sincerely believed that he drove Somapala's ghost up the jak tree. But it was mere bluff on his part to have said that he saw the branch of the tree shaken by the ghost. Neither he nor any one else could have seen that in the darkness of midnight."

## CAUSES

At this stage Piyadasa wanted to know from me the reasons why Leelawathy behaved like a 'possessed' person. I told him, "Leelawathy, like all villagers was brought up with superstitious beliefs about ghosts. Also she had a feeling of guilt about her illicit intimacy with Sarath, and the birth of her illegitimate son. She feared the ghost of Somapala more than the living Somapala himself, because she falsely believed that ghosts became omnipresent and omniscient the moment it left the body. It was Leelawathy's imaginary fear of Somapala's ghost, together with a subconscious awareness of her guilt that made simulate a 'possessed' state. If you can convince her that ghosts do not exist, the trouble will gradually stop."

I advised Appuhamy to leave Leelawathy alone as far as possible. I said that persons suffering from mental aberrations generally tend to exhibit them when there are others to see and hear them. Piyadasa and Appuhamy left, though not fully convinced by my explanations. Three weeks later on a Sunday, I visited Appuhamy's house in the company of Piyadasa. I was told that Leelawathy became normal two weeks ago.

## RESURRECTION

In January 1947 I left Richmond College, Galle to join St. Thomas College, Mount Lavinia. In March that year I received a letter from Mr. Piyadasa saying that Somapala has arrived home alive. He was captured by the enemies and taken prisoner of war. After the armistice, he was set free, and came to Ceylon with two other fellow prisoners.

The telegram received by Leelawathy five months ago was the result of a mix up on the part of the authorities. Since Somapala was missing after an encounter with the enemy, it was thought that he was killed in action.

I concluded my reply to Piyadasa with a remark, "Now it is possible to get possessed by the ghosts of living persons also!"

## Chapter 23

## THE GHOST OF TIME PAST

It was bedlam in Aron Singho's house. An 'evil spirit' was making life miserable for Aron Singho, his wife Podi Hamy and their only daughter Premawathy for the last eight months. "Thovil" ceremonies, five times repeated, could not chase this spirit from their house.

Sands and stones were thrown everywhere. Pots, pans, cups, saucers and glass tumblers were smashed on the floor. Flames from oil lamps were blown off even when nobody was near-about. Hair from the daughter's head was cut off by unseen hands. Letters written by the spirit fell into the house from nowhere. Objects flew about in the air. Clothes kept locked up in the cupboard were cut with scissors. Mysterious writings appeared on the walls. Sand was put in boiling rice.

In response to an appeal by D. Y. Ranasinghe of Kosgama, to get my help to lay the ghost at Aron Singho's house, a party of pressmen left Colombo on Monday 25th November 1963 with myself and my wife. On the way we stopped at the Migoda Mahavidyalaya to make enquiries about the route to Panaluwa where Aron Singho lived. The principal of the school Mr. P. S. Gunasekera and a friend of his Mr. P. Weerasinghe volunteered to pilot our car to the haunted house.

We branched off from the High Level road at the Migoda junction and stopped at the 3rd mile post on the Panaluwa road in front of a Tea Boutique. We were told by the villagers who had collected there that we have to walk about half a mile through paddy fields and rubber estates to reach Aron Singho's house.

From the day the news about the maddening manifestations in Aron Singho's house spread in the neighbouring villages, the business in this wayside tea boutique had improved steadily. Throughout the day there was a continuous stream of men, women and children going to the haunted house to satisfy their curiosity. This tea boutique served as a wayside rest for them. While we were driving along the Panaluwa road at slow speed, the villagers on the way recognised me as they have seen my picture several times in the newspapers. During the few minutes we were getting ready to start our march, a fairly large crowd collected round us.

Our party marched in single file, lead by Gunasekera and followed by the crowd. While on the march, a sudden scream from my wife startled the crowd. Two village women among the crowd helped my wife to pull out two leeches from her leg amidst hearty laughter. We reached Aron Singho's house at about 3.30 p. m.

## HAUNTED HOUSE

Aron Singho's small and new house was in the centre of a plot of land planted with rubber. The first thing we noticed as we entered the house was the bold writing with charcoal on the front wall in Sinhalese 'This house is haunted'.

"This was written some two months ago by the ghost. There are more writings on the walls inside the house," said Aron Singho, and took us inside. We entered into the bigger of the two rooms of the house. There were writings with charcoal on all four walls of the room. Though all the writings were in Sinhalese with numerous mistakes, there were a few isolated English letters scribbled here and there. Some of these English letters were inverted and a few others reversed showing that the ghost was not proficient in this foreign language, but was just trying to imitate. In some places the writings in Sinhalese were one on top of the other, and not decipherable.

## POLTERGEIST

Aron Singho and Podi Hamy jointly started giving a description to me of all what had occurred in the house since the mysterious manifestations started.

"It all started some 8 months ago," said Aron Singho, "First some sand fell in this room from the roof. A few days later stones started falling. Some stones were of the size of half-bricks. Later, plates, cups and saucers started flying about in the air. Even if they were locked up in the cupboard, they were thrown out. The ghost has broken 15 cups and saucers. It has broken many earthen pots by dashing them on the ground. We have seen pots being thrown out of the kitchen even when no one was in the kitchen. The ghost goes wherever our daughter Premawathy goes.

"On many occasions the flames from the oil lamps have been blown off by unseen mouths, even when the doors and windows were closed to prevent wind blowing them off. We got down famous 'kattadiyas' from all parts of the country. Although five 'thovil' ceremonies were conducted by different parties, the trouble continued. The last thovil was conducted three days ago. Premawathy's hair was cut by the ghost on five occasions."

At this stage Podi Hamy opened a box and brought out a paper parcel containing the long tuft of hair which once adorned Premawathy's head. It was long and thick enough to make a full-size wig.

"The ghost used the kitchen knife to cut the hair. It is only when she heard the knife dropping on the ground with the lock of hair that she knew her hair had been cut by the ghost. She cried loudly when this happened. When we rushed to her help we too saw both the knife and the lock of hair on the ground.

## DOMESTICS

"A good number of my sarees and Premawathy's frocks kept locked up in the cupboard were torn by this ghost", continued Podi Hamy, "The ghost makes dolls with pieces of cloth torn from my sarees. Some pieces are used for making patterns for jackets.

''Chilly, salt and scraped coconut were seen scattered on the floor one day. On many occasions we had to go without food because sand was put in the pot of boiling rice. Once a plate of rice was snatched off from Premawathy by a pair of disembodied hands. Clothes which disappeared from the cupboard were later found in the attic. The ghost drops letters giving instructions as to how the dolls it has made are to be treated.

"When Premawathy was sent to the residence of her uncle Ranasinghe, the ghost also accompanied her. While she was there, the ghost left a letter on Ranasinghe's table threatening to break his clock unless Premawathy was sent back to her parents. The ghost broke the feeding bottle of Ranasinghe's baby by crushing it between the bed and the wall.

"Shells of rubber seeds were thrown into the coagulated rubber latex. When people crowd in and around the house, the ghost throws stones at them. Sometimes remarks about named persons are written on slips of paper and thrown at them."

## INVESTIGATION

It was a difficult task to control the vast crowd which was surging into the house. They were anxiously waiting to see the ghost I was going to catch. Most of them would have thought that I would come out of the house with the ghost held by its neck! Unless the crowd goes out it was not possible for me to start my investigations.

To the surprise of all in our party, the whole crowd cleared out of the house when I came out and ordered them to do so. They marched out like a company of soldiers at the command of its captain. Wally was in quick action- with his camera, and lights flashing in all directions.

I conducted my investigations seated in the inner room. I allowed only three more persons to be with me in that room—My wife and Tillekaratne to act as scribe and Mr. Gunasekara, Principal of Migoda Widyalaya to act as interpreter.

The three inmates of the house were questioned by me individually. When one person was questioned, the other two remained in the outer room. I insisted that they spoke only about things which they have actually seen with their own eyes, and not what they have heard from others. I started with Aron Singho and finished with Premawathy. Among other things the following facts were revealed during the enquiry.

EVIDENCE

Aron Singho is 62 and his wife Pody Hamy 54. They were married in 1948. Pody Hamy was barren. They adopted Premawathy when she was 15 days old. They do not know who the real father of the girl is. The real mother did not want this child to live. Premawathy is 12 now. She is very backward in studies. Though 12 she is only in the Third Standard. She hasn't the physical growth of her age and has not attained puberty.

Premawathy has no friends and playmates either in the neighbourhood or at school. She keeps aloof from other girls. Other children who, according to Podi Hamy "are badly brought up" are not allowed to come to this house and "spoil our child".

Premawathy was never told she was an adopted child. They brought her up as their own child. Some eight months ago she came back from school with tears in her eyes. She said that her classmates were teasing her saying that she was an adopted child. But Aron Singho and Podi Hamy consoled her saying that those girls were telling lies. As the school girls continued to tease her she started disliking the school and finally refused to go to school.

PREMAWATHY

When I started questioning Premawathy I adopted entirely a different attitude. I spoke to her in a soft and endearing way with a smile on my face. I made her look at the tip of my nose. At this stage I signalled all others except my wife and Mr. Gunasekera to leave the room. After about 30 minutes Premawathy was sent out and her parents were called in again. Ten minutes later all came out.

I got out into the courtyard and addressed the large gathering in the garden. I said, "Henceforth there will be no trouble in this house. Aron Singho has spent more than Rs. 1000 on 'kattadiyas' to drive away a ghost which was nowhere in this house. All the incidents which took place in this house were the actions of a mentally sick inmate. That person has promised me not to repeat them in future. If the trouble starts again the remedy is in treating that person by a mental specialist, and not in resorting to 'thovil'. Man in his primitive stage thought that all physical and mental diseases were caused by the possession of 'evil spirits', and his remedy was 'witchcraft'. Today only persons in primitive state of mental development will resort to witchciaft to cure such diseases."

Amidst loud cheers from the vast crowd we left. At the special request of Mr. Gunasekera, we stopped for a few minutes at his bungalow at the Migoda Mahavidyalaya.

## ANALYSIS

While taking part in the High Tea served by Mrs. Gunasekera I told the other members of the party how Premawathy became a poltergeist thus:—

"It was a great mental shock for a girl of Premawathy's age to learn that the father and mother she loved so much were no more hers. The trauma made in a pre-adolescent girl by the loss of a person of affectionate love is as deep as the one experienced by a post-adolescent girl by the loss of a person of sexual love. This traumatic frustration made her a schizophrenic.

"Probably Aron Singho and wife brought up this child in isolation from neighbours to prevent them from telling her the real story of her genesis. This isolation has made her grow up into an artificial introvert.

"Premawathy herself was cutting her hair because of her unconscious desire to look like other girls in the school. Although her physical age was 12, I found her mental age not more than six or seven. Like other girls of 6 and 7 she had a desire to play with dolls, but she was denied that luxury. Hence she was tearing her mother's sarees and making dolls with them.

"Her backwardness in studies was due to her poor intelligence. From her real mother's attempt to abort her when she was in the foetal stage, I take it that during the first fifteen days of her life she might have been neglected and discarded as an unwanted child.

"Hei retarded physical and mental development, and her infantile ailments can be attributed to extreme malnutrition during the first few days of her life. The extent to which she can be reverted to normality depends on the tactful and understanding treatment by Aron Singho and his wife.

"I am sure all of you might have been listening with awe and distraught to those incredible eerie stories jointly narrated by the parents. I did not give any credence to what they said. I am used to hearing such incredible stories wherever I have gone for investigations.

"Inmates who believe that their houses are haunted live under spell of fear, and are subject to self-deception. Under such conditions they attribute all inexplicable acts where the actors deny responsibility, to the haunting ghost which is not there in reality. They become deeply disturbed and distraught, hence no value can be attached to their judgment .

"During my individual investigation today, neither Aron Singho nor Podi Hamy mentioned anything about such un-natural occurrences like objects floating in the air, disembodied hands, unseen hands, unseen mouths, the ghost following Premawathy etc."

## Chapter 24

## *A GHOST IN LOVE*

On 1st June 1962 I read in a newspaper the story of a haunted house in the hamlet of Retiyala in the Bulathsinhala police area where an 'evil spirit' was regularly writing love letters to a young unmarried woman, and was responsible for various mysterious occurrences.

It was reported that the blade of a coconut scraper was thrown at the newspaper correspondent when he visited the house on 31st May 1962. A crumpled letter was dropped from nowhere on his back.

Several attempts by 'kattadiyas' to drive the spirit away during a period of four months have been in vain, and the inmates of the house lived in constant fear, for often the spirit resorted to violence.

Sixty-two-year-old farmer Delgahage Podi Appuhamy and his wife, Missi Nona lived in this house together with their three sons and two daughters. The presence and the activities of the 'spirit' in the house was felt in January that year when they lost money from the drawers of the almirah.

### ESCAPADES

Gradually the 'activities' increased and the spirit began to throw stones, upset tables and chairs, dash pots and pans on the floor and drew pictures on the walls. The rice ration books of the whole family have been torn to shreds, and the family had no means of drawing their weekly ration.

When there was scarcity of dry fish in the country, this 'haunted' house alone in the area was supplied with excellent 'fishes' by the spirit, but nobody dared to taste it.

When cooking was over the ghost was glad to help itself to as much food as it wanted. Podi Appuhamy's wife claimed to have seen on several occasions cooked rice being served into a plate by unseen hands, and from the plate rice moved into an unseen mouth. When hoppers were prepared in the mornings, no sooner a hopper was taken out of the baking pan than it flew up across the air never to return. On one occasion the inmates of the house saw a large number of hoppers hidden among some old mates.

To visitors to the house the 'spirit' often gave orange, barley and cigarettes. The bottles of aerated water were dropped or rolled on the floor in front of the visitors, but no person was seen about.

## LOVE-LETTERS

The 'spirit' was reported to be specially interested in the 16-year-old Mai Nona, the eldest unmarried daughter of Podi Appuhamy. Once when she was taken ill, she was given all kinds of Ayurvedic medicines by the 'spirit' but she did not use any of these medicines.

Off and on the 'spirit' had been writing love-letters and throwing them at Mai Nona. Sometimes these letters were left by the 'spirit' under her pillow at night, and at other times they were tucked inside her blouse. All the letters were written on sheets of paper torn from single-ruled exercise books. The characters, though similar to Sinhalese, were not legible and decipherable. There were pictures of human beings too drawn in the fashion of child art. One such letter was thrown at the newspaper correspondent when he was there.

He saw a tin of powder flying from one room to another, and a bottle of sugar being dashed on the floor. At one stage the 'spirit' threw the blade of a coconut scraper at him, but it missed him and struck an iron bar of the window and dropped on the floor. The 'spirit' also stole a number of flash-bulbs from a bag of his.

## AT NIGHT

On certain days the chairs and other furniture in the house were taken away by the 'spirit' while on some other days things from other people's houses were brought to this house. At night the inmates of the house were not allowed to sleep in peace. Doors were opened at night and the inmates were pulled out of their beds. The ghost appeared to the mother one night and called her out, but when she came out to the courtyard it vanished.

Sometimes swords and knives were placed against their necks when they were asleep. 'Kattadiyas' succeeded in keeping the spirit out only for three days. On the fourth day it came back and resumed its usual pranks.

## VOLUNTEERED

On reading this story of the haunted house in the newspaper I contacted the newspaper correspondent concerned, and volunteered to investigate the case and prove that all the incidents in that house were the doings of a Schizophrenic, and not of any 'spirit'. I wished to keep the date of investigation a secret, as I wanted to avoid an inquisitive crowd collecting there.

On 5th June I travelled 33 miles from Colombo and held a three-hour investigation at this haunted house at Ratiyala. After the investigation I told the large crowd assembled there that I had been successful in tracing the member of the family responsible for the troubles, and that particular member had given me a solemn promise not to repeat them in future.

## A SECRET

I wished to keep the name of that particular person a secret for some time for obvious reasons. This was the shortest and clearest case out of the numerous similar cases I had handled successfully in the past.

I reached Ratiyala at about 3 p.m. accompanied by my wife, two journalists and a photographer. There had been a big rush of inquisitive people from all parts of the country during the past few days, and at the time of my visit too there was a crowd of over 300 near the 'haunted' house.

First of all I requested all the people to leave the compound and wait beyond the fence of the garden, leaving only the inmates of the house within. The crowd was co-operative and waited three long hours, outside the garden without causing the slightest disturbance during the investigation.

Next all the members of the family were introduced to me, and I started interviewing them one by one. A quiet spot under a coconut tree was selected for the purpose, and the father of the family was called first to give 'evidence'.

Altogether five members of the family were interviewed while my wife assisted in taking down notes. The investigation revealed the family history, domestic troubles, family enemies, personal problems and all other details necessary for the purpose. I insisted that I wanted evidences only about those things seen by each of them independently.

Ultimately it was found that nobody had seen some of the mysterious happenings such as "hoppers flying up in the air, cooked rice going up into unseen mouths, visitors being served with orange, barley and cigarettes by the 'spirit', furniture coming from the neighbouring houses" etc., reported to have been seen by the inmates of the house.

## THE LETTERS

With regards to the letters written by the 'spirit' I established clear proof that they were the work of the inmate I suspected. All the members of the family were asked to write on a piece of paper, and the writings of one person, who was completely illiterate, tallied perfectly with the letters of the 'spirit'. It was a xenoglossal attempt of that illiterate person to imitate Sinhalese scripts.

Xenoglossy or glassolalia is a mental aberration in which a psychotic person attempts to read, write or speak a language unknown to him or her. Such expressions do not represent any real language extant or extinct, and no coherent meaning can be obtained from them although a few real letters or words may be included here and there. In those 'love-letters' written by the schizophrenic, an attempt is made to imitate the morphology of Sinhalese characters, but no coherent words or meaning could be had out of them.

At the end of the investigation I asked the person concerned not to repeat the 'activities' in future, and the person concerned gave a solemn promise. I on my part undertook not to divulge anything about this promise even to the members of the family.

Finally I invited all the people outside to come near the house, and I made a short speech. I said that there would be no more trouble from the 'spirit' from that day onwards, because I had handled and solved the case on a scientific basis instead of resorting to the mumbo-jumbo of 'kattadiyas'. I said that it was a pity that the poor farmer had to spend over Rs. 1500 on 'thovil' ceremonies and 'kattadiyas'.

The eldest son of the family, Dolis Singho thanked us for the great help rendered them. After partaking the 'kurumba' liberally supplied by Podi Appuhamy, we left amidst loud cheers from the vast crowd.

## POSSESSED

Four days later a car-load of people from Ratiyala arrived at my residence. The mother of the family, Missi Nona, with her hair let loose and the whole body violently jerking," was led into my bungalow. She was held firmly by her eldest daughter Mai Nona and the eldest son Dolis Singho. Missi Nona was made to- sit on a chair. The physical jerks became more and more violent with the head swinging round and round, and finally she collapsed with a fiendish shriek.

Dolis Singho said, "Sir, you have only stopped all the 'activities', but you have left the ghost still in our place. Last night it got into our mother's body".

At this stage I called Mai Nona aside and told her that the time for breaking my promise to her had come. I said, "The only way to cure your mother is by telling her the whole truth about all what had been happening in your house for the last four months". Mai Nona gave a silent consent.

When the mother regained her consciousness I explained to her and Dolis Singho how and why the 16-year-old Mai Nona became a poltergeist, and what sreps should be adopted in future to keep her sober.

Missi Nona went home happily followed by her children.

## ANALYSIS

Missi Nona became hysterical and behaved like a possessed person as a result of her hallucination originating from her delusional belief in spirits. Unlike the village 'Kattadiya' who generally satisfies the inmates of the house by pretending to drive away the non-existing ghost by sending it up a neighbouring tree or a herd of animals. I left the house without 'driving' away the spirit although I stopped all its 'activities'. The idea was lingering in Missi Nona's mind, and it was no wonder that she got 'possessed' as a result of her own imagination.

## Chapter 25

## *A SADHU'S MAGIC CURE!*

It started with an attack of splitting headache, which lasted for four days. With the cure of the headache, began a mania for reading newspapers. All her waking hours she spent in reading newspapers,- but the progress she made in reading was nil. Day in and day out, from the morning till evening, she sat on the same chair on the verandah with a sheet of paper in hand. The whole day she read the same page; no, the same paragraph; no, no! the same word. Her eyes were glued to one and the same spot in the paper.

With great difficulty, her mother had to pull her out of her favourite chair to force her to take her meals. She lost her appetite, and refused to take food. The result was that she gradually got thinner and thinner, and finally became anaemic.

Saraswathy was a bright student at a girls' school in Jaffna. While she was studying in the 'Cambridge Junior' class, her brother Kandasamy, an equally brilliant student, was in the 'Cambridge Senior' in a boys' school near Saraswathy's.

### MIGRATION

Father, Mr. Ramanathan the Chief Clerk in a Government office in Colombo was waiting till Kandasamy finished his schooling, to bring his wife and the two children to Colombo to stay in the house he had newly constructed at Wellawatte. Saraswathy's education was not a major concern. After all, she had to be given in marriage soon, and it was easier to find a suitable young man in Colombo than in Jaffna.

Thus, the whole family migrated to Colombo in 1945. Kandasamy joined the University, and eventually obtained an Honours degree in Science. He secured an executive job in a flourishing foreign firm.

Saraswathy stopped her schooling and was awaiting matrimony. It was in 1947 that the first symptoms of melancholia appeared in her. As days went by there was a radical change in her melancholial introversion. She started talking to herself, with occasional fits of laughter.

Kandasamy who used to visit me occasionally for an evening chit-chat, expressed a wish that I saw Saraswathy and expressed my opinion. One day, Saraswathy was brought to my residence. While the parents and Kandasamy waited in the drawing room, myself and my wife had a prolonged conversation with Saraswathy in another.

Later I told Kandasamy and his parents that the girl was fast entering into a neurotic state, and recommended matrimony as a possible solution.

## SADHU

A few days later, Ragupathy, an assistant clerk under Mr. Ramanathan suggested consulting a famous 'sadhu' regarding Saraswathy's case. This 'sadhu', according to Ragupathy, was reputed to possess great mystic powers. He had cured many 'incurable' diseases given up as 'hopeless' by expert doctors.

Once, when a party consulted him about a missing person, he gave the name of a hotel in a distant town where he could be found. On enquiry it was found, to the surprise of all concerned, that the missing person was living in one of the rooms in that hotel.

Mr. and Mrs. Ramanathan finally decided that this 'sadhu' should be consulted. Next day Ragupathy arrived at Ramanathan's house with the 'sadhu' The Ramanathans received the holy man with due respect and devotion, and made him sit in the drawing room, on a chair on which a white sheet was spread for the occasion.

Clad in a flowing yellow robe, with long beard, and hair tied up in a spiral knot on the head, and sandalwood paste spread on the forehead with a red 'spot' in the centre, the 'sadhu' cut a saintly figure.

At the outset Mr. Ramanathan gave a detailed description of his daughter's troubles. Saraswathy was called in and made to stand before the 'sadhu'.

## POISON

The saintly man closed his eyes and remained in deep meditation for a few minutes. Then he opened his eyes and said, "This girl is under the spell of a charm. A jealous woman, a close relative of the girl's mother, has poisoned her through a liquid food. It can be extracted only by conducting a 'sarpa pooja'.

Saraswathy was sent back to her room. A consultation between the parents and the 'sadha' resulted in fixing the date for the 'sarpa pooja'. The 'sadhu' dictated a long list of articles to be got ready for conducting the pooja.

After Ragupathy and the 'sadhu' had gone, there was a heated argument between Kandasamy and his parents. Kandasamy said that all what the 'sadhu' said was a lot of nonsense and the best thing to do was to show Saraswathy to a mental specialist and get treatment for hysteria. But the parents were not prepared to throw away the valuable advice given by the saintly 'sadhu' and accept (he one given by the immature boy.

The parents spent hours together trying to identify the woman who poisoned Saraswathy. By process of wild guessing and elimination they arrived at an innocent cousin of Mrs. Ramanathan at whose house the Ramanathans attended a party some months ago.

"Yes, I am sure", said Mrs. Ramanathan, "she must be really jealous because our son is drawing a higher salary than her eldest son although both of them have the same qualifications". Ramanathans dccided to have nothing to do with this family in future.

## POOJA

The 'sadhu' arrived on the appointed day with a cloth bag hanging from his shoulder. He entered the room specially arranged for conducting the 'pooja'. Two plantain leaves were spread in front of the 'sadhu' who sat cross-legged against a wall. A brass pot with a husked coconut in its mouth was placed in the centrc. Just behind it a lighted coconut oil lamp. The other articles on the plantain leaves were rice, puffed rice, flowers, crushed rice, plantain fruits and a small earthen pot half-filled with milk.

The 'sadhu' pulled out from his bag a dried-up stem of a wild creeper, shaped like a snake with zig-zag bends in -it, and placed it leaning against the pot containing the milk.

Saraswathy was made to sit on a low stool in front of the 'sadhu'. Continuous chanting by the 'sadhu' went on for about twenty minutes. The first half of the pooja was terminated by the recitation of a few Sanskrit 'slokas'. The second half commenced with the 'sadhu' conversing with his deity.

He was seen jotting down on a piece of paper the message he received from the deity. The actual 'extraction' of the poison from Saraswathy's stomach took place during the later part of the second half of the pooja.

Smoke from powdered incense sprinkled on burning cinders in a tray filled the room. The atmosphere was solemn and serene. Except for his chants and whisper to his deity nobody uttered a word in the room.

Saraswathy was seated motionless. The incense tray with smoke rising from it was circled round her head thre-times. Then the 'sadhu' gave one end of a thirty-inch-long thread to be held in Saraswathy's mouth by biting it. The other end was kept dipping in the milk.

## POISON OUT

The chant now became louder and louder. The 'sadhu' took a handful of jasmine flowers from his bag and held them in his left hand With the right hand he sprinkled a few of these flowers on Saraswathy's head. Then he dropped one flower each on the various victuals on the plantain leaves including the milk in the pot. Then he took the snake-like stick in his right hand and passed it repeatedly from Saraswathy's head to the milk pot.

During this process the colour of the milk began to change into pale blue first and into deeper blue later. After about five'minutes, the 'sadhu' declared that the whole poison from Saraswathy was transferred to the milk. All in the room including the doubting Kandasamy marvelled at the miracle.

## INTERMENT

Saraswathy was made to stand up. The 'sadhu' blessed her by placing both hands on her head and said that she would have no trouble in the future.

While Mrs. Ramanathan was looking at her husband with a smile of satisfaction, the 'sadhu' called the servant who was standing in the room and gave the pot of blue milk to him and said, "While I conduct a special pooja here you take it to the back-yard and put in it as much cow-dung as you can pick with three fingers of your right hand. Make a pit in the garden. Hold the pot in both hands, face to the west, pour out the milk into the pit while you keep on looking at the sun, place the empty pot also in the pit and break it, and finally cover up the pit."

Soon after the servant left the room with the pot, Kandasamy also went with him. He took the pot and the milk from the servant and kept it in his cupboard and locked it up, and told him not to tell about it to any one.

## REWARD

The 'sadhu' collected all the victuals into his bag and was getting ready to depart. Mr. Ramanathan and wife worshipped him and begged of him to let them know how they should reward him for the great help rendered.

"I don't charge anything. In fact, I don't touch any money with my hands. If you are very keen that I must accept something you may put some twenty five rupees in my bag", replied the 'sadhu'.

Mr. and Mrs. Ramanathan held a conversation in whispers and decided that the saintly man deserved much more than he himself suggested. They folded a fifty rupee note and inserted it into his bag.

Kandasamy accompanied the 'sadhu' to the bus halt. After putting the 'sadhu' into the first bus going towards Pettah, he crossed over to the other side of Galle Road and took the next bus to Mount Lavinia to meet me and tell me about the miracle performed by the 'sadhu'.

Within a few minutes of the 'sadhu's departure I entered Ramanathan's house accompanied by Kandasamy, and walked straight into his room. Kandasamy took the pot of milk out of the cupboard and showed it to me.

DETECTED

After examining the colour of the milk, I called for another vessel. When the milk was decanted into the other vessel there appeared a partially dissolved blue ink tablet at the bottom of the pot. I picked out the ink tablet and gave it to Kandasamy. He ran out with the messy tablet to show his parents.

The repulsive reaction generated in Ramanathan and wife when they realised the fraud inflicted on them at a cost of fifty-odd rupees would have resulted in a murder had the 'sadhu' been anywhere near them.

Kandasamy felt humiliated and small before me for failing to detect the fraud when the 'sadhu' surreptitiously introduced the ink tablet into the milk along with the jasmine flower he put in ir during the pooja.

In my small speech to Kandasamy and his parents I said, "Just like a magician's trick can be- detected by a watchful eye, the frauds of a necromancist also can be found out if one is careful enough to watch even the minutest move. This 'sadhu' was a very clever and cunning person. His instructions to your servant to put cow-dung into the milk, to keep on looking at the sun while the milk was poured into the pit, to break up the pot, to bury the whole thing etc., were all sound precautions to prevent anyone detecting the ink tablet.

"There is a mistaken notion among ignorant people that charmed poisons can remain in the stomach for months and years creating mental troubles, and that they can be brought out by counter charms. It is a racket among 'kattadiyas' to play on the credulity of people and confirm such stories.

"I know of a Christian priest in Colombo who, like the village 'kattadiya' has set up a lucrative practice among the gullibles for counter charming 'charms'.

"Physiologically, all poisons entering the alimentary canal will eventually find their way out through urinary excretions. If they are undigestible substances, they automatically are removed with the faeces, without in any way affecting the central nervous system, and thus the mind."

Enraged Ramanathan traced the hideout of the 'sadhu' next day with the help of Ragupati and got back the full fifty rupees under threat of reporting to the police.

It took two days to remove the blue stain from my fingers.

## Chapter 26

### *LATHA AND HER MYSTERIOUS LOVER*

RANASINGHE and wife were the happiest of parents in Padukka that Sunday. Their eldest daughter Latha's photo appeared in two newspapers with descriptions of how she captained her school to victory in a net-ball match against a reputedly strong team from a Colombo school.

Describing the play the sports correspondent in a Sunday paper wrote, "Tall and Pretty, Latha was the centre of attraction. From start to finish it was a case of Latha and the ball".

It was not a case of "good at games and bad at studies" with Latha. At the last prize distribution at her school she carried away all the prizes for the S.S.C. class including the much-coveted prize for general proficiency. Her name was specially mentioned in the Principal's report as an ideal student who had contributed richly to the life of the school during the two previous years. As the Head Girl of the school she was highly respected and loved by all other students.

Latha was also an object of crazy admiration among the boys in the neighbouring boys' school. She was in her sweet sixteens with vital statistics fit for a beauty queen. She was recognised as the best-dressed girl in her school.

Latha's school profited financially by her popularity among boys. Tickets for entertainments at Latha's school sold like hot cakes in the boys' school. The senior boys of that school knew very well that they get their money's worth by feasting their visual and auditory senses when Latha sang or danced on the stage.

#### FATHER'S PET

At home she was the pet of her father. Although Ranasinghe's income from his clerical job in a Government department was not very high, he spent lavishly on Latha. Both her father and mother took pride in seeing their pretty and clever daughter dressed in good, though not expensive, attire. Ranasinghe had two more daughters aged 12 and 10. He had no sons.

Latha's "bad time" seems to have started from the day she finished her S.S.C. Examination. After this she never had a chance or liking to step into her school which she loved with all her heart.

Mrs. Ranasinghe noticed a sort of melancholic expression on Latha's face from the day her examinations were over. She seemed to have lost all interest in life. Her present indifferent attitude towards everything was in marked contrast to her usual active life Both the father and mother became anxious about Latha's changed behaviour.

## METAMORPHOSIS

Mrs. Ranasinghe noticed that Latha was getting into new frocks every morning for three or four days at a stretch. On the fifth morning when she was changing her frock, mother asked why she was changing her clothes every day. Latha replied that the one she was wearing had torn at night.

The next day too when she was getting into a new frock, her mother examined the one she- discarded and found it torn in two places. In about two weeks' time Latha had exhausted all her frocks in the wardrobe. All those dresses which she wore once were torn in many places. As most of the tears happened to be in 'awkward' places, Latha aid not like to wear them during the day.

On being questioned by the father and mother how her clothes were being torn every day, Latha replied that they occurred at night without her knowledge.

As Ranasinghe did not like his pretty daughter to be seen by others in torn frocks, he got a few new ones made for her. But those too met with the same fate. Mrs. Ranasinghe began to lose her patience and began to scold Latha, and on one occasion she was given a thundering slap on the cheek.

This made matters worse, and from that day things took a different turn. Next morning Latha woke up from her sleep with larger holes in her frock. It appeared that portions were cut off with a pair of scissors. As these tears too were in places which needed maximum covering, and since there were no other frocks in the wardrobe, Latha started patching up the torn ones and wearing them again.

## GHOSTS

Mr. and Mrs. Ranasinghe now suspected that it was the work of some mysterious evil spirits. So they consulted a kattadiya from Ginota. This kattadiya with a party of five others came home and performed some poojas and "manthras". They buried some kind of white stones at the four corners of the house. They went back with their stipulated fee of Rs. 200.

Instead of stopping the trouble, the charm had only adverse effects. From that day onwards holes in the dress were not made with scissors but with fire brands. Till this time all the damages to Latha's frocks happened only at night, and on those she was wearing. But now burnt holes started appearing on her dresses which were hanging on pegs and cloth-lines. By the end of the second month Latha was dressed in tatters both day and night.

## PRISONER

Because of the conditions of her dress, Latha remained in her closed room constantly like a prisoner. Even her food was served in the room. The only occasion she went out of her room was when she went to the lavatory.

She gave up the habit of taking her daily bath. She also gave up the earlier practice of mending the torn parts of her dress, because most of them had several patches one over the other. Mother kept the scissors, knives, blades and box of matches out of Latha's room.

At this stage Ranasinghe consulted a Light-Reader. The 'Light-reader' said that the spirit of a dead maternal uncle of Latha was in love with her, and was responsible for doing all those things. Mrs. Ranasinghe vehemently opposed that suggestion because no brother of hers had ever died. Moreover she resented the repulsive idea that a brother of her's would fall in love with his own niece.

All these days Latha used to say that she did not know how her dress used to get torn at night. But now she started complaining that a spirit comes to her at night fights with her and tears, cuts and burns her frocks.

One morning she got up from her sleep and started crying rather loud. Both the father and mother rushed into her room to see tufts of Latha's hair cut and strewn on the bed and floor. At this ghastly sight Mrs. Ranasinghe could not control her sorrow and bursted out weeping. Latha said that the spirit came twice the previous night. During the first visit it scratched all over her body, and bit her. During the second visit the ghost started cutting her hair off.

## YANTHRA

As things were getting from bad to worse, Ranasinghe wrote to his brother-in-law Stanley Perera of Moratuwa to bring home the famous exorcist-priest from Pillyandala. Ranasinghe got a new frock made to be worn by Latha when Mr. Perera was to bring the priest.

Finally, when they got news that the priest would be arriving the next day, Mrs. Ranasinghe decided to give Latha a forced bath. In spite of her protests Latha was taken into the bath room with great difficulty, and persuaded to remove the torn frock from her body. The mother could not help weeping at the sight of red scratch marks all over Latha's chest and thighs. There were traces of dried blood in a few of those scratches. On Latha's right biceps there was distinct mark of a bite.

Elaborate preparations were made to receive the priest the next day. Next morning Latha was made to put on the new frock specially made for the occasion. The priest accompanied by Mr. Perera came at about 10 a.m. After a prolonged chanting of 'manthras' and incantations the priest tied some 'charmed threads' on the right ankle and neck of Latha. A talisman (yanthra) containing a few drops of oil said to be 'Vishnu Raja

Thaila' was tied on Latha's arm. The priest was given alms and his fee.

For about two days after the enchanted threads and the 'yanthra' were tied on Latha there was no trouble. But it started on the third night with severer intensity.

Mr. Perera of Moratuwa (Ranasinghe's brother-in-law) in a letter gave my name and address and asked Ranasinghe to meet me by appointment.

A day later Ranasinghe met me at my residence, and gave a vivid description of Latha's present troubles and past history. Myself and my wife visited the Ranasinghes at 'Lathanivasa', Padukka, at about 11 a.m. on a Sunday. Without wasting much time on formalities we were taken into Latha's room and were offered two chairs. Latha was seated on her bed. All except Latha were asked to retire from the room.

Latha was dressed in the new frock specially made for the priest's visit. At the outset my wife asked Latha to show her some of the torn frocks. Latha pulled out. a heap of them from a cupboard. There were about fifteen. All of them were badly torn. Five had burns. About eleven had patches of repairs. Holes and tears were seen only in front of the frocks.

Latha, in spite of her poor eating and mental agony for the last two months, looked a perfect specimen of health. She was pretty, fair-skinned, with curly hair—now bobbed as a result of the ghost cutting them short. When she smiled, which she appeared to be doing always, dimples appeared on both her cheeks. Her smile also exposed a small gap in her upper front teeth. Although she was only sixteen, she had the physical development of an eighteen-year-old girl.

At my request my wife examined Latha privately. She then gave me a description of what she had observed on Latha's body. There were five scratches on her chest, all on the left side. Two scratches were visible on the inside of her right thigh. The mark of a bite was clearly seen on the biceps of the right arm four inches below the armpit. In the outer row of the dental marks there was a small gap in the centre.

YOUNG MAN

I ordered Latha to lie down flat on her bed and relax completely. I fired a volley of questions in stiff tone, and demanded Latha's answers in quick succession. As a result of an hour's intensive questioning I gathered, among other things, the following information which is given in her own words: —

"A strong young man comes to me at night when I am asleep. I wake up by his caresses and kisses. He brings me presents in the form of chocolates, sweets and perfumes. After some moments, he asks me to go with him in a car waiting outside the gate. When I refuse to go with him he fights with me. During that struggle my clothes get torn. Sometimes he gets very angry and bites me.

"He has sharp nails, and scratches me with them. Whenever .I prevent him from tearing off my clothes he cuts holes in it.

"When he starts fighting with me he grows very big like a giant and carries me up in his arms. When I struggle he drops me on the ground. One day he cut all my hair with a pair of scissors."

When I asked Latha whether she has seen anyone like him before, she said, "Yes, he is just like Lionel, the

foot-ball captain of ___ .... school. I used to meet

him on my way to and back from school. Poor boy. he died in a car accident three months ago. He was such a nice chap that whenever our net-ball team went out to play matches he made it a point to be there to cheer us." When she said this I noticed tears on Latha's cheeks.

SUGGESTION

Under a hetero-suggestive spell Latha accepted responsibility for all the incidents such as tearing and cutting holes in the clothes, clipping off her own hair, setting fire to her dress and scratching and biting her own body. While in that state I made her promise that she would not repeat such acts again.

We came out of Latha's room after one hour and ten minutes. We sat to lunch with Mr. Ranasinghe while Mrs. Ranasinghe served. At the lunch table I explained, though not in full, the cause of the trouble and advised him to give Latha in marriage to a suitable young man, preferably a sportsman.

Today Latha is a happily married lady with two pretty children, a boy and a girl.

## ANALYSIS

When a news-reporter asked me whether I could give an explanation for Latha's behaviour I replied, "You should not forget the fact that Latha herself will be reading this article about her, and I have to be extremely careful to see that you do not write anything which would affect her married life. However, if you can interview me again two days hence, I may be able to help you."

At the interview two days later I told the reporter, "I met Latha and her understanding husband yesterday and talked over the whole matter with them. As both of them feel that a pseudonymous analysis of Latha's temporary mental lapse may be beneficial to the readers of your paper, while doing them no harm, they have given me liberty to use my own judgement. Hence, here are some of my explanations:

"Even if Latha had not accepted responsibility for those mysterious happenings, from the available evidence I would have come to the conclusion that she herself was doing them. She was a right handed person, hence all the scratches appeared only on the left side of her chest. If a 'ghost' was doing it, at least one or two should be seen on the right side also. The small gap in her upper incissors was duplicated in the dental marks left by the bite on her right arm. Holes were seen on the left cups of the brassiers because she was using right hand to do it.

"Throughout that period of two months she maintained that a 'ghost' was doing it because she believed it to be so. She, like most persons, was brought up from childhood wrapped up in nonsensical ghost stories. It is not unusual for persons with such ideas in their subconscious minds to experience such hallucinations. Moreover, as she was suffering from schizophrenia at that time she couid not have recalled to her conscious memory what she did as a different person

FRUSTRATION

"Then arises the question as to what made her become a schizophrenic. I **say it was purely the result of sexual** frustration. She was a healthy girl in the prime of her youth, probably with hyperactive sex glands. She was brought up in a very modest home away from the company of males. If she had brothers, she would have had opportunities of meeting the boys who came to meet her brothers.

Probably Lionel, the footballer, was the only young man with whom Latha had a chance of talking freely to. There is no doubt that both of them were sexually attracted to each other. Their prowess in games might have contributed to their mutual attraction. The fact that Lionel went to see all the net-ball matches captained by Latha is an indication that he derived great pleasure in seeing Latha exhibiting her sporting talent.

"Lionel's sudden death three months before was a big shock and a personal loss to Latha. She did not get a chance to brood over it during the first month of his death because she was preoccupied with her final S.S.C. Examination. From the day the examinations were over, the thought about Lionel began to torment her subconscious mind. It transformed her into a melancholic.

"The strong young man who came to her at night was her hallucinatory image of Lionel. His caresses, kisses, attempts to ravish, bringing of presents, invitations to go with him, carrying her in his arms etc., were really her wish-fulfilment.

"Cutting her hair short too was the result of a subconscious wish to present herself before her lover in more fashionable style. Cutting and tearing of her frocks to expose certain parts of her body was an expression of exhibitionism. Also it was a trace of masochism in her which made her scratch and bite her own body. She derived pleasure from such pains imagined to be inflicted by her lover.

"The man becoming like a giant during the struggle confirms my view that she had a fetish for a muscular manly man. That is why I advised the father to select a sportsman as her husband,

*N.B.*: While all the incidents in the above article are absolutely factual, for obvious reasons the names of persons and places are fictitious.

## Chapter 27

## *GHOSTS ON (& OFF) THE ROAD*

A very well-known and wealthy motorist, who was one of our pioneers in Sri Lanka and a great enthusiast, was the owner of a Delauny-Belleville many years ago. I have seen the car; it had a huge circular brass radiator, brass windscreen,folding hood and a brass luggage carrier.

The motorist had gone to the races at Galle and was returning late one evening to the Hikkaduwa Rest-House where he was staying. His car was full and he asked his chauffeur to sit on the luggage carrier. Thus the chauffeur was facing backwards and seated in the rear of the car. The motorist himself took over the driving.

Suddenly opposite the Dadalla cemetery all the lights went out. He stopped his car, and the chauffeur got out and re-lit the great big carbide lamps. The party then proceeded and when they got to Hikkaduwa the waited for the chauffeur to come from the back and open the car doors (this was the days when old world courtesy was functioning). As the chauffeur did not come round, the motorist, not very pleased, got out of his car and went to the back to find his chauffeur laid out on the luggage grid in a dead faint. The chauffeur was revived and came out with his story:

After the lamps had been re-lit at Dadalla and the ear proceeded, a figure in white kept on running behind the car. Each time the figure got close to the car it became bigger and bigger, and then two arms stretched out to seize him. When he shouted the figure retreated and became smaller and smaller. As his shouts did not reach the occupants of the car because he was seated at the rear and facing backwards, no help came to him, and then the figure came on again and again.

Quite unable to bear the horror of it the poor chauffeur became unconscious. The next thing he knew was being revived at the rest-house.

How many motorists have experienced this type of thing at Dadalla?

This story appeared in 1961 July issue of "THE RECORD", the monthly journal of the Automobile Association of Sri Lanka. The following story was also reported.

## GORAKANA GHOST

The Galle Road has another fatal spot. It is the cemetery at Gorakana. There stands a woman with a child under a tree. She greets a passer-by with a request for him to hold the child. If the passer-by shows signs of fear or accepts the offer and carries the chiid he dies. This happens only to the lone passer-by.

Motorists deserve a better fate, so they see neither the woman nor the child, but something makes them swerve at this spot and go over the edge. The number of accidents here is proof of this.

It is said that the use of as much bad language as possible in the loudest tone makes the woman disappear. She just cannot stand bad manners.

## KANATTE GHOST

The third story narrated by Mr. J. was of a foreign lady, involved in an accident at Rosmead Place when she was travelling in a taxi and died. Since then taxi-drivers passing the Lych gate at the Kanatte cemetery after dusk are halted by a 'white woman' who gets into the taxi and gives an address at Rosmead Place. When the taxi driver reaches the address he finds there is no passenger! Next time a taxi driver refuses a fare at the Lych gate at Kanatte cemetery you will know why.

## LETTER

Having read these three ghost stories. I wrote to 'THE RECORD": —

"It is rather surprising that you found it fit for publication such silly 'motoring ghost stories' as given in the July issue of THE RECORD. Surely such grandmother-siories, which are never verified and proved true, need not find a place in the pages of journals of the type of THE RECORD which are mainly meant to assist the users of a scientifically mechanised mode of transport of the modern age.

The fictitious nature of these ghost stories mentioned by Mr. J can be found by a careful reading of them. About the ghost of the woman and child at Gorakana he says, "If the passer-by shows signs of fear or accepts the offer and carries the child, he dies. This happens ONLY to the LONE passer-by. Motorists SEE NEITHER THE WOMAN NOR THE CHILD, but something make them swerve AT THE SPOT AND GO OVER THE EDGE. The number of accidents here is PROOF of this. It is said that the use of as much BAD LANGUAGE as possible in the LOUDEST TONE makes the woman disappear". (Capitals mine).

## ANALYSIS

An analysis of the above narrative brings out the following facts and raises certain questions:—

1. As it happens only to lone passers-by, there, are no eye-witnesses to these incidents.
2. The dead persons are the only one who could have told others what really happened. As dead persons are incapable of speech and writing, how was the conclusion that they died as a result of fear or of carrying the child, arrived at?
3. How did those, who are said to have survived after seeing the ghost, know that they would have died had they feared or carried the child?
4. The woman-ghost, like the Dadalla ghost, is capable of hearing although her ear-drums and the brain had decomposed long ago after her death!
5. Since motorists see "neither the woman nor the child" it is rather absurd to attribute their cars 'going over the edge' to the woman and her child who are not there.
6. Many car accidents at one and the same spot can better be a proof of the unsuitable nature of the road than the presence of ghosts. In other countries such a state of affairs would normally attract the attention of Road Engineers; but it appears

that in Sri Lanka it would bo a case for the 'katta-diyas' to rectify.

7. Can the effective 'bad language' to be used be in any language? If so, is the woman-ghost a multi-linguist? If not, are those passers-by who are not proficient in that particular brand of 'bad language' doomed?
8. Can Mr. J supply a list of the lone persons found dead at this spot during a sufficient long period? Coroners' inquest reports and or the local police station should furnish him with the necessary information.
9. Has Mr. J. taken into consideration the hundreds or even thousands of motorists who pass this way at night throughout the year without meeting with any accident? I am one among those.

With regard to the Kanatte ghost Mr. J. says, "Since then (the death of a foreign lady in a taxi accident) taxi drivers passing the Lych gate at the Kanatte cemetery after dusk are halted by a 'white woman' who gets into the taxi and gives an address at Rosmead Place. When the taxi driver reaches the address he finds that there is no passenger!"

Unlike the two other cases of DadaJla and Gorakana, where the persons concerned are no more living, there should be many taxi drivers now living in the city of Colombo who are said to have had the misfortune of taking the ghost of the 'white woman' to Rosmead Place.

It is not said whether the ghost of the 'white woman' appears dressed in her western costume or stark naked. If she is naked, it is not likely that the taxi driver would bodily accept a nude woman as fare, especially from the Lych gate of Kanatte cemetery. If, on the other hand, she was clad properly like a living woman, then we have to conclude that not only the dead woman has left her ghost behind, but the various items of her lifeless dress also have left theirs. The same applies to the 'white' dress of the Dadalla ghost who was capable of performing a race with the car although it had no bones and muscles. Or had it?

## ALIVE OR DEAD?

From this woman-ghost's reported ability to speak to the taxi drivers, one has to infer that her vocal-cords, lungs, mouth, tongue and the speech-centre of the brain are still functioning although these organs have decomposed long ago and merged with the soil of the Kanatte cemetery. Or could it be that ghosts develop some sort of built-in gadget for reproducing speech, and thus setting up the necessary air-vibrations to enable others to hear?

I am still waiting to meet at least one of the 'many' taxi drivers in the city of Colombo who are said to have had the misfortune to take the vanishing ghost to Rosmead Place.

Subsequently I spent two nights with another person till 2.30 a.m. each night at Kanatte seated in my car parked just outside the Lych gate. We counted a total of 21 pasengerless taxis passing up and down this spot. Not one was stopped by this or any other ghost during these two nights.

## Chapter 28

### *THE MERCHANT AND A MYSTERIOUS GHOST*

"Now who could be calling at this siesta hour", I wondered as I lay on my reading lounge, the quietude of my room disturbed by the incessant jangling of the telephone. I wasn't trying to receive the message by means other than telephone; but I could not resist a calculated guess. "It must be some troubled soul", I thought, and walked up to the telephone.

And troubled soul it was!

The voice that came over sounded breathless and excited. "I am Mr. Mihra here", it said, "There have been some very mysterious happenings in my house and I have been advised to consult you about it".

"What kind of mysterious happenings?" I asked.

"Well, for the past one and a half years I have lost various sums of money in my house. .

At this point I wasn't too sure whether the man at the other end had got the right number. What he might have needed was the police. But when Mr. Mihra continued, "I am inclined to believe that this is not the work of thieves ... I mean, not the work of human beings" I knew we were both on the right line.

### A FRANTIC MR. MIHRA

Later that day (Nov. 26th, 1966) a car drove upto 'Tiruvalla'—my residence. It was a frantic Mr. Mihra, together with his uncle, calling for help and insisting that I go to his house at once. A matter of life and death!

"Come, come in, Mr. .Mihra, sit down and calm yourself, and tell us all about the case", said I, beckoning them to the hall. Mr. Mihra, realising then that he had been rather precipitate, did as he was told.

He was a 33-year-old Pakistani textile merchant, who about one and half years earlier had lost Rs. 300 from a wad of notes amounting to Rs. 3000, which had been kept in his wardrobe. Later on there were further losses, until he thought it wise to consult a soothsayer.

Poojas were soon held and all manner of rituals were conducted; after which the soothsayer arrived at a very definite diagnosis of the case: Mr. Mihra's enemies in business were sending ghosts to create trouble in his home. Hie soothsayer rounded off his long drawn out ministrations by tying a thread round Mr. Mihra's hand. All would be well, he assured his client.

## JEWELLERY SET MISSING

And all was well—for three months. But early in the fourth month Rs. 200 vanished from the wardrobe. Then a few mornings later Mr. Mihra's wife complained that a jewellery set was missing. It was worth about Rs. 3000.

For three months Mr. Mihra's financial security had hung on a thread, so to speak,—a charmed thread. But now it had snapped. And was all that charmer's threadwork a mere yarn?

Mr. Mihra dared not answer that question until he had found some new protection against his ruthless business enemies. Anyway, the distressed man didn't have long to wait There was plenty of occult help available, .and many names were mentioned. Of these, Mr. Mihra picked a powerful kattadiya from Ambalangoda.

This kattadiya—a veritable sandow of the occult world—meant business, but neither he nor his familiars were destined to meet and do battle with the black spirits hired by Mr. Mihra's business enemies.

He went into the case very carefully and arrived at quite a different view of the trouble. "Yes, there was a spirit," he said, though it wasn't a hired hoodlum spirit but a highly respected dead member of Mr. Mihra's family. In life this person had been deprived of some of his dues, and he had carried that grudge with him beyond the grave.

## TO ASSUAGE THE SPIRIT

Of course, the spirit could be assuaged. The kattadiya was quite certain of that, and he advised an extra large thovil ceremony. Food and other offerings were to be regularly kept for the spirit in a special room.

the burly, mustachioed kattadiya organised the ceremonies with teutonic thoroughness. The devil-dance was a screaming success—the biggest of its kind ever seen in the area. And when it was over and done with, Mr. Mihra was greatly relieved, except that one little nagging thought still bothered him: what if the kattadiya had misinterpreted the situation; and what if the so-called spirit of a dead relative he had been feeding every day in a special room turned out to be none other than the hoodlum spirit hired by his terrible business enemies? Wouldn't he be opening himself to a crippling attack from the nether world?

While these questions were working his mind to fever-pitch, Mrs. Mihra's wife had a fainting fit that seemed to confirm her husband's worst fears.

With time, the fainting fits kept on recurring and Mr. Mihra was getting really desperate. But about that time certain other manifestations occurred, which, in a way helped to lessen their fears and divert their attention.

## MYSTERIOUS LOVE LETTERS

The Mihra householders had now begun to find in odd corners old cigarette-tins full of bones, human hair, limes, copper coins etc., Mr. Mihra's own discoveries were even more surprising. There were love letters deposited in his coat and trouser pockets and, on one occasion, in an account book. Altogether he came across eleven such love letters—ten in English and one in Tamil—over a period of several months.

The central thought in all these passionate notes was a plea to Mr. Mihra to accompany the writer to India. In other words, to elope. Here are the excerpts from the letters:

"Darling Mihra, you should not be frightened... I will do anything for you.. . Don't forget June 14th _______ You must come every night.. . Don't tell your wife.. . We can fly by plane.. . Darling Mihra, loving kisses.. . I am happy you came last night . . Don't write your name in the letter ... I like your singing. ... Come tomorrow night. . . . Mihra and Saree."

Other elements in these letters that drew attention were the frequent reference to the date June 14th, and the invariable subscription—Mihra and Saree.

Mr. Mihra may have been a little flattered by the epistolary attentions of this amorous astral being. But surely, it could not be his dead male relative, unless he had changed sex after death! Or could it be that having been regularly fed and ritually cared for in a special room, his dead relative had now developed a most unnatural desire for him? The third possibility was much more alarming: It could well be that his business enemies might have changed their tactics, and were now baiting him with a love line.

Without further ado Mr. Mihra got down a third charmer—a Muslim man with a very big reputation. He, too, was a specialist in thread-work and he tied threads for all the members of the household—Mr. and Mrs. Mihra and their two children, Mrs. Mihra's mother, and Mrs. Mihra's four brothers and four sisters.

Mr. Mihra was somewhat sceptical about efficacy of these threads, and, in fact, his wife's worsening condition soon confirmed his doubts: her fainting fits were occurring more frequently, so much so that he began to wonder whether the spirit had gained complete control over her.

## THEIR HOPES IN A DREAM

Now something effective had to be done quickly. Mr. Mihra and his friends and relatives were getting quite frantic; and so they called in a fourth kattadiya, who conjured up hope of a solution in a rather novel manner. Having completed series of poojahs, the charmer announced that one member of the family would soon have a very significant dream, which would indicate to them the source and the cause of the troubles.

But months passed by and yet nobody dreamt anything of significance. Meanwhile, more money was being lost, more love letters and charm-materials were being found, and Mrs. Mihra was having fainting fits one after the other.

Then in the third month after the fourth charmer's ministrations, Mr. Mihra's mother-in-law came up one morning with a very meaningful dream. She said' that in the dream she saw two thugs and a small boy attempting to forcibly enter Mr. Mihra's house. Her son-in-law promptly challenged them and a fight ensued. She finally prevailed upon him to stand aside and let the thugs and the little boy take what they wanted from the house.

The kattadiya was summoned without delay; but he appeared to be somewhat baffled about the identity of these dream-figures. Anyway, he performed a lime-cutting ceremony, after which he made himself scarce.

## NOW A LIGHT-READER

Months passed by and the situation was again becoming intolerable. Mr. Mihra's wife was fainting at the most unexpected moments. More charms and mysterious and embarrassing letters were being found, and more money was being lost.

Besides all that, there was one other development: Mr Mihra had lost all faith in kattadiyas and he now turned to a light-reader for help. This-was the fifth professional occultist on the scene.

He, like one of the previous charmists, required a special room for his work, though not for the purpose of feeding spirits. The room was duly provided and the light-reader proceeded to place a candle in the middle of the floor, after which he requested that a young boy or an 'unattained' girl should be made to look at the candle flame.

Mrs. Mihra's 12-year-old sister was the chosen flame-gazer. She was instructed by the light-reader to gaze intently at the flame untill she could see not one but "two flames. When after some minutes the girl exclaimed that two flames were visible, the light-reader urged her to keep on gazing until ten flames were visible. The girl did as she was told and then excitedly cried out that she could see many flames.

Now the girl was faithfully doing his bidding; the atmosphere was growing hypnotic and electric, and at the psychological moment the light-reader recommended her thus: "Now you will see your dead grandfather's face in the flames!"

The girl gazed on and on. Then in a whisper she was heard to say: "I see him, I see him" Charmer: "Now you can ask your grandfather who the culprit is."

Whereupon the girl shouted out, "I can see two thugs and a little boy. They are breaking into our house!"

## STAGGERING COST OF IT ALL

With that the charmer relaxed himself, and the light-reading was over. He probably had no idea that the girl's vision was very similar to Mrs. Mihra's mother's dream. Yet, he was definite in his analysis: "These thugs are the spirits who are doing all these. They are being sent by your enemies to harm you, To counteract their charms we must offer a very powerful pooja".

Mr. Mihra was obviously sick to the gills with all these poojas, thovils, thread-tyings, light-readings and lime-cuttings. Nevertheless, he acceded to the man's request.

About this time, the distracted Mr. Mihra happened to tot up the sums of money he had expended on charmers; and the poor rich man, on checking the figures, nearly had a fainting fit himself.

The total was Rs. 15,000!

One and a half tormented years had gone by; about nine-hundred rupees a month, on average, had been spent on the Island's best sorcerers—but the Mihras' involvement with spirits had only deepened.

## A PETRIFYING SIGHT

On that night of stock-taking when Mihra totalled up his expenditure, he naturally had very little sleep; and the next morning—November 25th, 1966—he woke up and went to work.

Meanwhile, Mrs. Mihra had decided to take a morning bath. In the bathroom she remembered that she didn't have her veil with her. So she went back to the bedroom to fetch it and there she came upon a petrifying sight. What looked like smoke was seeping out of all the orifices of her almirah. But was it really smoke? Could it not be the ethereal fingers of a ghostly being or beings?—those fendish hoodlum spirits, perhaps? Mrs. Mihra's mind reeled at the fearsome possibilities and then she screamed and screamed.

Her mother, brothers, sisters, neighbours—they were all there in a trice. The almirah was literally torn apart and the old adage pToved correct again: no smoke without fire.

Nearly all the clothes she owned were in that almirah and they were now an acrid, congealed mass of what were once uncrushable terylenes, scinillating bri-nylons, the silkiest Kashmeres and the most gorgeous Benares and Kanjeepurams.

## ENTER—MR. MIHRA'S UNCLE

Everybody was awed and thunderstruck. Had the ghostly robbers now turned to vandalism? In the weird circumstances that attended the case, that was certainly a pertinent question, but one that was never voiced either in that smoke-filled room or outside it.

For now there came into the scene a strong personality, who took complete control of the situation. It was Mr Mihra's uncle. With growing concern and rising anger he had watched and heard of the black-magical and necromantic antics that were being performed in his nephew's house. The gullibility and superstition of his relatives in general and Mr. Mihra in particular had appalled him beyond belief. But he, on principle, minded his own business for one and a half long years. Now, however, the time had come to step in and initiate some sensible action, even if it involved the seeming usurpation of the position of chief householder in Mr. Mihra's house.

Soon after the fire was discovered a frantic phone-call was made to Mr. Mihra's textile establishment, and when the distraught man came rushing in, his uncle all but assaulted him and declared that he was taking control of the situation.

They would begin, he said by consulting Dr. Kovoor—immediately. The flabbergasted Mr. Mihra was ordered to make a call to me and a while later uncle and nephew called at my house. I agreed to go and investigate the case.

## RATIONALIST TECHNIQUE

When I arrived at the scene, the crowds had dispersed and I was free to use the classic rationalist technique of individual questioning in order to dispel mass-hysteria and sort out the facts from the fiction the individual acts and experiences from the nebulous mass of superstitious beliefs and fallacious reasonings that so often colour a subject's thinking.

I decided to deal with just four people from a household of over 15. These were Mr. Mihra's mother-in-law, two of Mrs. Mihra's brothers and Mrs. Mihra herself.

The procedure was quite simple. Each of them was called into a room singly and was requested to write down certain phrases on the dictation of mine. These phrases were chosen by me from the mysterious love-letters that had been found in the house. A prime production in the case.

When this rather unusual dictation test was complete, I asked each of the interviewers to tell me individually and privately all that he or she had seen and heard in connection with the strange happenings in that house.

Soon after the interviews were over I turned my attention to the specimen of hand-writings I had before me; and having repeatedly scrutinised and checked the four pieces of paper against the love letters of diverse scripts that I also had with me, I boldly discarded three of the specimen writings.

## A WORD MISSPELT

One swallow, it is said, does not make a summer, and one clue does not prove a case. But a significant clue necessitates a follow-up which might reveal a linkage with a whole chain of vital evidence.

The main clue was a word misspelt. The word was "AFTER". It occurred thrice in the love letters as "UFTER", and there also was "UFTER" in one of the specimen writings! Thus the culprit was indicated. But could the culprit be apprehended on the basis of that one bit of evidence?

Furthermore, from the severe rationalist point of view it appeared that no corroborative facts could be firmly fettered to the case at that stage, for interviews had revealed nothing. But certain nebulous clues that could not be pinned down to a clear hypothesis were now dancing a complex arabesque in my mind. These clues were key words from the love letters:—

"June 14th,.... Saree.... June 14th,.... We can fly by plane to India.... You must come every night.,.. June 14th, Mihra and Saree....“

And yet as a rationalist and a man of science, how could such light fantastic conjectures that were forming in my mind be given any credence?

## THE MOMENT OF TRUTH

I was precariously perched on a tenuous line of logic. I was holding on to a word misspelt as my balancing stick, and the only way to get across, I realised was not by the cautious approach of science but that of art—the vaulting intuitive art. I must first point out the culprit and then seek for the still unrevealed motives. I had come to the bedevilled house that night at 9.15. Now the time was close on one o'clock and I had decided, on the basis of my hypothesis, that the moment of truth had arrived for Mr. Mihra.

Thereupon I gently called nephew and uncle aside to another room, locked the door, and then expressed my view of the case: "Mr. Mihra, it is your wife who has been responsible for all that has happened here."

Mr. Mihra was dumbfounded at first; but on recovering from the shock of that revelation he began to heatedly dispute the diagnosis.

I listened with deep sympathy to the husband's protestations; for how, in truth, could any normal man accept that kind of damning statement about such a dutiful wife, such a ravishingly beautiful, modest and good-natured young woman!

## UNDER HYPNOSIS

But at this stage Mr. Mihra's uncle made an unexpected intervention: "You bloody fool", he told his nephew with some heat, "you accepted every weird word those money-grabbing kattadiyas had to say. But now you are trying to argue. Why can't you accept what this learned gentleman has told you?"

The uncle continued regardless: "Mr. Kovoor, my nephew and I will do whatever you want us to do. I shall see to that."

Mr. Mihra now looked somewhat lacking in spirit. The crisis had passed and I took the opportunity to instruct them to bring Mrs. Mihra in two days time to my house for a session of hypnosis and mental rectification by means of suggestion."

They were also strictly enjoined to say or do nothing that would in any way give Mrs. Mihra cause to suspect that they were aware of her doings.

On the appointed date uncle, nephew and wife turned up at "Tiruvalla"—my residence. The two men were asked to wait in the hall while myself and my wife accompanied Mrs. Mihra upstairs.

The young woman readily responded to my hypnotic suggestions. I had her full co-operation. In fact, while in the hall, she had repeatedly implored me to really help them in their trouble. Mrs. Mihra was now fully relaxed and in a couple of minutes she had lapsed into the deep-trance state.

## UNCONSCIOUS CONFESSION

And then the floodgates opened, as she truthfully answered my questions.

Yes, it was she who had written the love letters; she had prepared the charms; She had put a match to the almirah_ in fact, she was the author of every 'psychic' manifestation in that thrice unfortunate house.

When the unconscious confession was complete, I proceeded to spell out to her carefully and repeatedly the all-important suggestions that would prevent her from continuing her surreptitious activities in the house. On and on I went, phrasing and re-phrasing my suggestions until I thought it time to wake her up.

But now followed the ordeal of mine!

The hypnotic 'open sesame'—a count of three and a twist of the toe would not work. It had been a never failing means of unlocking suspended volition and bringing patients back to reality; but Mrs. Mihra wouldn't —more correctly couldn't—wake up.

I was not unaware of the reasons for this almost deathly oblivion. Yet, that certain knowledge did not prevent the breaking out of a cold sweat on my body.

## THE ANODYNE OF SLEEP

The fact of the matter was that the purgation of Mrs. Mihra's psyche had been an overwhelming experience, and both body and 'mind' were now seeking the anodyne of deep sleep in order to effect re-intergration. That was obviously her condition, and myself and my wife decided that our patient would need a lot more of nature's healing balm before she was ready to face normal life again.

So, during the next two hours or so I busied myself downstairs with Mr. Mihra. There were a lot of loose ends to be tied up and Mr. Mihra could, no doubt, assist me.

Who for instance, was Saree?

At first Mr. Mihra found it rather difficult to **answer** that question, but on my insistance he did.

## SAREE—LOVED AND HATED

Saree was an attractive Indian nautch-dancing girl who was the sole performer in a spell-binding carnival side-show that had been touring the Island.

Mr. Mihra happened to know the manager and proprietor of that outfit, and in playing host to them he might have been a trifle too hospitable to Saree, the prima donna whose nightly dance macabre at a carnival nearby was the talk of the town. But that is another story.

Muslim women, as we all know, lead very sequestered lives, and it is not unlikely that Mr. Mihra's renewal of old acquaintances—though evidently above board—might have given rise to suspicions.

The next question was: When and how did Saree leave for India?

"On June 14th by plane," said Mr. Mihra.

## THE PRICE SHE PAID

The recurrent phrases that danced arabesque-like in my mind—"Don't forget June 14th ... we can fly by plane . . . You must come every night. . . .”—were the key phrases in the mysterious love letters. And now they seemed a little less mysterious in the light of the dawning revelations.

So Mrs. Mihra was Saree. She loved and hated Saree. But more anon of the why and the wherefore.

Now there was one final question to be asked. I wanted to know whether Mr. Mihra was supporting his wife’s mother and her children. And when I was answered in the negative the case was complete. I had with that last question, laid my finger on a very rational motive. It was money and family feeling.

Mrs. Mihra cared deeply for her brothers and sisters. They had to be fed, clothed and educated. But where was the money to come from?

On the other hand, Mr. Mihra’s marriage arrangement did not envisage such encumbrances. He was marrying a beautiful young woman—not her mother and children.

And there was the rub.

But money had to be found somehow by Mrs. Mihra. And find it she did—at a price.

The price Mrs. Mihra paid was in guilt—guilt-edged insecurity—and it so kept weighing her down that every now and then something had to give inside her; and what ‘gave’ were her senses: She had frequent fainting fits and thereby temporarily relieved herself of the unbearable burden of deceiving—and thieving from—her husband.

## DOUBLE-EDGED FEELINGS

As time went on, the psyche’s makeshift attempts to even the scales of conscience ceased to be effective. Occasional airy fits and loss of wits wouldn’t any longer tip the balance. And so a more weighty internal solution was seized upon by the unconscious mind. It took the form of a suspicion of infidelity on the part of Mr. Mihra.

The conscious mind, of course, would never admit such a thought into its rational presence; but it could, with a high degree of finesse, be made to manifest itself in the guise of a subjective reversal of roles.

And this Mrs. Mihra did by imagining herself to be Saree—the sweet nautch-dancer who was once brought to their home by Mr. Mihra.

Furthermore, this makeshift solution could hardly hurt anyone. After all, she wasn't really accusing her husband of infidelity. What was happening was that a dissociated part of her mind was imagining itself to be a nautch-dancer Saree. And Saree was having an imaginary affair with Mr. Mihra. Hence the ghostly love letters.

But Mrs. Mihra's feelings towards Saree were evidently double-edged: When she wanted to be Saree she wrote love letters to her husband and when she hated Saree she set fire to her sarees and laid charms in the house.

For Mrs. Mihra the main consideration was that in the economy of her personality and psyche she could, by the acted-out innuendo of infidelity, lessen the high cost of her guilt. Until, ofcourse, its exorbitant demands led her to weider methods of justifying the act of stealing money from her husband.

Fortunately at this stage I took up the case.

After the long two hours of sleep, Mrs. Mihra was woken up. She was a normal and happy woman once again.

The expressed their gratefulness to me for dispelling all their troubles with just four interviews, a dictation test, and a few well-chosen hypnotic words.